JOHNNY DEPP'S ACCIDENTAL FIXER

HOW A HOLLYWOOD SLEUTH SAVED A PIRATE'S HONOR.

By Paul Barresi

Copyrights © By Paul Barresi
All Rights Reserved
Published by: WritersClique.com

Acknowledgements

Special thank you to my editor Anne Quinn and representative Adam Smith with the WritersClique for helping me bring the publication of my book to fruition.

My profound thanks and appreciation to Jean Barresi, Megan Fox, Rob Sheiffele, Wendy Harvard, TUG, Angenette Levy with Law & Crime, Dr. James Hopkins, Joe Menandro Cabrera and Johnny Depp's *'consigliere'* Adam Waldman, for encouraging me to tell my story.

Preface

Those who followed the Depp v. Heard defamation trial might think they know the full story but beneath the surface lies a narrative shaped by shadowed truths and unspoken realities.

In July 2019, I was hired by Amber Heard's legal team to probe into the life of Johnny Depp. The *'Aquaman'* actress's request was clear: validate her claims against her ex-husband, the globally renowned *'Pirates of the Caribbean'* star, known for his charismatic and at times, controversial persona. I believe that to truly understand someone, one must start at the very beginning where the seeds of the present are sown in the soil of the past.

This book chronicles my journey—an investigative foray beyond the glaring lights of Hollywood into the veiled corners of personal histories. Initially met with silence, resistance, and warnings, I found conventional avenues of inquiry blocked. Doors remained closed, calls went unanswered, and sources recoiled at the prospect of revealing truths that could burn bridges or ignite scandals.

Faced with these challenges, I reverted to the essence of all investigations: start from the beginning. What I unearthed about Johnny's tumultuous upbringing and the industry that both fueled and consumed him, provided profound insights into the man behind the celebrity veneer. This narrative digs deep into the shadows of Hollywood, guided by official documents, interviews and an unwavering quest for the truth.

The discoveries made were illuminating, troubling, and undeniably fascinating, compelling me to share this story. From the depths of hidden truths to the peaks of public scrutiny, *Johnny Depp's Accidental Fixer* gives you a front row seat through the dark alleys of a glittering world where the facts are more intriguing than fiction.

Paul Barresi

Forewords

"Johnny Depp's Accidental Fixer" is a fascinating true story about an old-school Hollywood PI at the center of the biggest trial since OJ Simpson to capture the public's attention. To get to the truth, a person must find and believe the evidence surrounding an allegation. That's what Paul Barresi's job was and is exactly what he did."

--Megan Fox

Megan Fox is a political commentator, satirist, award-winning journalist and author of Believe Evidence: The Death of Due Process from Salome to #MeToo

"Johnny Depp's Accidental Fixer" is a real page turner...I couldn't put it down! Paul Barresi's book goes deep -- giving a rare, inside look, into the world of a Hollywood fixer. The Accidental Fixer is ripe for a Netflix series."

--Rob Sheiffele

Rob Sheiffele is an Emmy nominated producer, writer and development executive with long standing positions at E! Entertainment Tonight, Extra and The Doctors.

Table of Contents

Chapter 1	The Op-Ed Controversy 1

Chapter 2	Shadows and Spotlights 13

Chapter 3	Hollywood's Hidden Truths 23

Chapter 4	The Hunt Begins 40

Chapter 5	The Viper Room History 52

Chapter 6	The Rocky Road 80

Chapter 7	Unraveling the Tangled Web 96

Chapter 8	Baruch the Mooch 101

Chapter 9	Roots of Resilience 112

Chapter 10	The Threads That Bind 124

Chapter 1
The Op-Ed Controversy

In the ever-turbulent world of Hollywood, where fame and scandal are often intertwined, few stories have gripped the public's imagination as intensely as the legal battle between Johnny Depp and Amber Heard. This saga filled with accusations, trials and revelations, began with an op-ed—a piece that would ignite a firestorm and set in motion a series of events that captivated audiences worldwide.

It was December 2018, a time when Hollywood's glitz and glamour were overshadowed by a brewing storm. Amber Heard, known not just for her roles on the silver screen, but also as Johnny Depp's ex-wife, had penned an op-ed poised to send shockwaves through the industry. This wasn't just any op-ed; it was a declaration, a narrative laden with implications and a harbinger of the legal battles to come.

In crafting this piece, Amber sought the counsel of Eric George, a renowned attorney and a member of the

American College of Trial Lawyers. George's task was clear yet daunting: to refine Amber's op-ed in a manner that would shield her from legal repercussions while allowing her to voice her alleged experiences. This was a high-stakes game, a balancing act between expression and implication requiring the utmost precision and care.

Known for his meticulous approach and deep understanding of the legal landscape, George was aware of the gravity of the situation. He scrutinized every word, every sentence of the op-ed, ensuring it was fortified against potential defamation claims and legal challenges. His expertise was crucial in navigating the complex interplay of public perception and legal constraints.

The op-ed, published on December 18, 2018, in the *Washington Post*, under the auspices of the American Civil Liberties Union [ACLU] was more than just a piece of writing; it was a catalyst. Amber presented herself as a figure representing domestic abuse, a stance that resonated with many but also raised eyebrows. Though Depp's name was never explicitly mentioned, the intimations were obvious, especially to those who had followed the couple's highly publicized relationship.

The publication of the op-ed set the entertainment world abuzz. It was a bombshell that landed with a resounding impact reverberating across media outlets and social platforms. The inferences of the article were far-reaching, painting actor Johnny Depp, beloved for his portrayal of eccentric characters like Captain Jack Sparrow and Edward Scissorhands, in a controversial light.

The Me-Too Movement played a significant role in the backdrop of Heard's op-ed and the subsequent legal battle. Following its publication, Amber became a symbolic figure. The movement gained considerable traction and public attention, creating a favorable climate for her allegations. As the investigation unfurled it was like setting sail on the fierce winds of the Me-Too Movement.

The initial public opinion seemed to sway in Amber's favor, resonating with the movement's call for accountability and support for survivors of abuse. As the trial date approached and the case unfolded, the tides began to shift and public opinion became more divided. It felt akin to a ship stuck in the doldrums of windless waters near the belt of the equator.

The enduring tailwinds that had initially propelled the movement and Amber's claims began to wane. The outcome of the trial with Amber's loss to Johnny, not only impacted her personally but also had broader implications for the Me-Too Movement. It could be argued that the stunning verdict handed down by the Fairfax County, Virginia jury favoring Johnny Depp, marked the beginning of a decline in the movement's influence.

In this complex landscape, those who admired Amber rallied to her side, while Johnny's supporters fervently defended him. It became a case that divided public opinion, with each revelation and piece of evidence scrutinized and debated by the public and the media.

The fallout was swift and multifaceted. Fans and detractors alike were drawn into the narrative, taking sides and voicing their opinions in a saga that bore all the hallmarks of a Hollywood blockbuster: fame, fortune, and scandal.

The op-ed became a focal point of debate, not just about the allegations it contained but also the broader issues of domestic abuse and the responsibilities of public figures in highlighting such issues.

In response to the contributor column, Johnny Depp took legal action. In March 2019, he filed a defamation lawsuit against Amber, seeking fifty million dollars in damages. The stage was set for a legal showdown that would rival any dramatic screenplay, a battle that would unfold in the courtrooms and the court of public opinion.

Amidst this legal maelstrom stood the *'Aquaman'* actress, a woman who through her action had unwittingly thrust herself and Johnny into a trial by public scandal. Despite the backing of substantial financial resources and a formidable legal team, the weight of the situation was palpable. The op-ed had not only sparked outrage among Johnny's fans but had also ignited a fierce debate on domestic abuse and the role of celebrities in societal issues.

Struggled with the fallout of her decision, Amber found herself embroiled in a conflict that was rooted in more than just her allegations against Johnny. It was a battle that spanned legal, social, and personal fronts, a conflict steeped in complexity and high stakes.

In the shadowy corridors of Hollywood, where crisis and controversy are often the norm, there exist individuals, adept at navigating such treacherous waters. These are the fixers, the behind-the-scenes players who are called upon to untangle webs of controversy and shed light on obscured truths.

My entry into this high-profile case was a testament to this hidden world of Hollywood. With more than three decades of experience conducting challenging investigations for Hollywood luminaries like, Arnold Schwarzenegger, Tom Cruise, Sylvester Stallone, Gerard Butler and Eddie Murphy, I had established a reputation as the go-to-guy, highly skilled in sifting through the secrets that smolder beneath the red carpet.

On July 7, 2019, Amber Heard's attorney Eric George contacted me, seeking my expertise as a legal consultant for his client. My mission was straightforward yet formidable: to delve into the life and history of Johnny Depp and uncover evidence of his alleged physical abuse towards women. It was a challenging assignment, one that would demand all my investigative experience and know-how.

While sitting in the luxurious Beverly Hills offices of Brown George Ross LLP, I was aware of the magnitude of the task ahead. The term *"Ivory Tower lawyers"* took on a new meaning as I surveyed the sprawling city below, where dreams are made and broken, and the boundaries between truth and imagination frequently becomes indistinct.

The strategy meeting with Amber's legal team was a convergence of legal minds and investigative prowess. The key to this investigation lay in uncovering tangible evidence: videos, photographs, admissions of guilt—anything that could substantiate Amber's claims against Johnny. The challenge was immense, requiring a meticulous and thorough approach to gather credible evidence and piece together the complex puzzle of Depp's life.

With the gravity of the task weighing heavily on my mind, the drive back to my home office in Rancho Cucamonga was a contemplative one. I knew that the road ahead would be fraught with challenges, but I was ready to embark on this investigative journey.

My tools were databases, public records, official documentation, archived legal filings and the internet; all of which became invaluable allies as I scoured them for information about Johnny, his family, friends, ex-girlfriends, co-stars, associates and employees. My goal was to leave no stone unturned, to gather every piece of credible information that would shed light on the truth behind the allegations.

Amid this unfolding legal drama, a key figure emerged in shaping the course of Amber's defense: Rick Schwartz Esq, Eric George's right-hand man. As midnight approached, I delved into the articles sent by him, each offering a glimpse into Johnny's world. From stories of late-night altercations to accusations of violence, every article added a piece to the intricate puzzle of Johnny Depp's life. The narratives painted a picture of a man who was multifaceted and enigmatic—a man whose life was ladened with contradictions and controversies.

Known for his comprehensive legal expertise, Schwartz played an instrumental role in the case. He litigated a wide array of high-stakes disputes, ranging from trade secret misappropriation to sexual misconduct and from defamation to tax controversies. His experience with sophisticated investors and technology startups, coupled with his work on constitutional challenges under the First Amendment, made him an invaluable asset to Amber's legal team.

In addition to his litigation practice, Schwartz's role as the Secretary and General Counsel for the Simon Wiesenthal Center, highlighted his commitment to justice and ethical legal practice. His career trajectory, including pivotal roles as a trial attorney for the United States Department of Justice, underscored his capability to handle complex legal challenges.

Schwartz's involvement was crucial in relaying precise instructions and expectations between Amber and the investigative team. He was the linchpin in the communication chain, ensuring that Amber's desires were clearly articulated and pursued with diligence and strategic acumen.

The next day brought new challenges as Schwartz sent evidentiary material for my review. From emails to videos, each piece of evidence offered a potential lead, a clue that could unravel the mystery surrounding Johnny Depp. The task was daunting, requiring a discerning eye to separate fact from fiction, to analyze the evidence and to uncover the truth.

Sifting through the dossier I was struck by the complexity of the case. The *'Transcendence'* actor's life was a maze of relationships, incidents, and contradictions that defied easy categorization. The investigation was not just a legal case; it was a journey into the heart of Hollywood where secrets lay concealed, and facts were obscured. My investigation into Depp's life, led me down paths I never expected, uncovering truths that would shake the very foundations of Hollywood's glittering facade.

Contemplating my quest, I knew that the road ahead would be long and arduous. I was up for the task and determined to uncover the evidence that would finally bring clarity to this convoluted saga. The investigation was more than just a legal case; it was a journey into my undisputed turf, Hollywood's underbelly-- where the line between hero and villain is often blurred and fame and scandal are inextricably linked.

This journey into Depp's world was not just an investigation into allegations of abuse; it was an exploration of the very nature of celebrity and the power dynamics that define the entertainment industry. It would reveal the difficulties of human relationships, the fragility of reputations and the often-harsh realities of fame.

As I delved deeper, I came to realize that this case was about more than just proving or disproving allegations. It was about understanding the human condition, about peeling back the layers of a story that had captivated the world. It was about finding the truth in a world where truth is often elusive, where appearances can be deceiving and distinguishing between what is real and what is imaginary is a challenge.

The investigation reminded me of the power of the media, the role it plays in shaping public perception, and the responsibility that comes with that power. It caused me to reflect on that shadow box of a place called Hollywood, where concealed skeletons are closely guarded and truths are often hidden from view. A world where behind the glitz and the glamour, nothing is ever quite as it seems.

I knew that my findings would have far-reaching implications, not just for Johnny Depp and Amber Heard but for the worldwide entertainment industry. It was a case that would shine a light on the darker corners of Hollywood, the power struggles for dominance and the battles that take place behind the scenes.

This was a story of fame and fallibility, of power and vulnerability, of truth and deception. It was a story that would captivate the world, a chronicle that would be told and retold, analyzed and debated. And at the heart of it all was the search for truth, a search that would take me on an expedition through the labyrinthian world of La La Land, and jettison me into the lives of two of its most famous inhabitants.

Forging ahead, I knew that the journey would be filled with twists and turns, with revelations and discoveries that would challenge everything I thought I knew about the case.

Reflecting on the arduous nature of the investigation, my experience traveling the often-convoluted paths of trial by scandal, came to the fore. The challenges faced in

Paul Barresi

these cases though different in context, had equipped me with the resilience and insight necessary for the task at hand.

The Depp v. Heard lawsuit presented a unique scenario. Comparable to the rare *'Fujiwhara Effect,'* I found myself caught between two storms, interacting in an intense dance around me-- representing one celebrity Amber, against another, Johnny.

Caught between two storms

Image Credits: (Photo by JIM LO SCALZO / POOL / POOL / AFP) (Photo by JIM LO SCALZO / POOL/POOL/AFP via Getty Images) and (Photo by Cliff Owen/Consolidated News Pictures/Getty Images)

Chapter 2
Shadows and Spotlights

The unfolding saga between Johnny Depp and Amber Heard, with its intricate weave of accusations and trials, mirrored the Hollywood dramas I had grown up idolizing. As I stepped into this whirlwind, it transcended being just another case. It marked a confluence of my past and present—a pirouette with the shadows and spotlights of a world I had both dreamed of and dreaded.

Raised in a close-knit, lower middle class Italian American neighborhood on the outskirts of Boston, my upbringing was nestled within a community where solidarity among Italian Americans formed a bulwark against the social oppression we faced.

The 1950s was a time when jokes, jeers, and name-calling like *"ginny," "greaseball," and "wop,"* were commonplace, painting my childhood with the harsh strokes of ethnic discrimination. This backdrop of adversity extended into my household, where violence was more frequent than words of affection.

In the tapestry of my family's history, two figures stand prominently: my mother Miriam and my father Nick. Their physical allure was undeniable, a trait that neither lacked nor went unnoticed. My mother balanced her life between her familial duties and her part-time work as a cocktail waitress at the Wagon Wheel, a local haunt that served as an escape from the tempestuous reality of her marriage.

My father's predilection for alcohol, coupled with his indignant demeanor when inebriated pushed my mother further away, making her susceptible to the attentions of other men-- overtures she found increasingly difficult to resist. My father was a government civil servant who worked as a welder at the U.S Naval shipyard in Boston's oldest neighborhood; the waterfront town of Charlestown. After work, he routinely found solace, not at home, but at the bottom of a glass. What began as a single beer would invariably spiral into a night of excessive drinking.

A womanizer by nature, the head of the household I grew up in was buoyed by flirtatious glances. His recurrent nights out and not coming home sometimes for two or three days, were not solely driven by pursuits of one-night stands. Once alcohol clouded his judgment beyond a certain threshold, if my father wasn't bar hopping and chasing women, he'd find himself engaged in bare-knuckled, barroom brawls. These events would often lead to bruises, stitches and sometimes even jail.

Raised in a hard-knock life and scarred further by the fierce battles he fought while serving with the U.S. Marines during WWII, my father never shied away from a fight. The physical confrontations he engaged in were as vital to him as the air he breathed. He thrived in these moments of conflict, drawing from them a perverse form of sustenance.

My father's fury was not reserved for the outside world alone. My childhood bore the brunt of his violence in a more personal and harrowing manner. He frequently unleashed it upon me and my mother, embodying the very definition of a physically abusive patriarch.

A searing memory from when I was eight years old encapsulates the terror that my father was capable of. In a drunken rage, ignited by my mother's act of pouring his last bottle of beer down the kitchen sink, I watched in terror as he unmercifully punched her about the face and head until she fell lifelessly to the floor like a mangled ragdoll. The image of my mother's eyes swollen shut and her lips gushing with blood is as vivid today as it was nearly seventy years ago. This terrifying experience was a stark, indelible reminder of the darkness that dwelled within him, casting long shadows over my formative years. The slightest missteps could unleash his wrath. One evening during supper I accidentally spilled a glass of milk, which resulted in an immediate backhand across my face.

My father's methods of discipline were far from conventional parental punishments. Instead of administering traditional spankings, he opted for swift closed-fisted punches to the top and side of my head, leaving welts and swelling that could not be seen. The intensity of his violent manhandling and forceful blows often caused me to see flashes of light. I literally saw stars and occasionally I would momentarily blackout.

The verbal assaults mirrored the physical ones. My father would relentlessly degrade me, his words echoing the violence of his actions, belittling me as *"rotten and no good,"* insisting that I would *"never make it in life."*

This cycle of abuse was unyielding, allowing me only brief periods of respite. My father's beatings and torment cast an unpromising shadow over my life. It is within this context that my mother's actions must be understood. It wasn't a mere wandering eye that led her into the arms of other men, but the push of my father's own indiscretions and neglect. The complexities of their relationship marked by love, betrayal and the struggle for understanding, wove a poignant chapter in the narrative of our family's history, a chapter that speaks to the resilience of the human spirit in the face of adversity.

The ceaseless physical and emotional torment that shadowed my upbringing was an unrelenting presence, a relentless daily ordeal. From the tender age of two months until I reached the precipice of adolescence, my health was perpetually compromised. I was diminutive for my age, always embroiled in a battle against chronic bronchitis and recurrent episodes of pneumonia that plagued most of my formative years.

My education unfolded within the austere halls of Catholic institutions from the first through seventh grade where my frequent tardiness and struggles to achieve mere passing grades were met with scant patience from the nuns.

Sister Earlene my seventh-grade educator, remains an indelible figure in my memory. Her tall slender stature, those piercings, pale blue eyes and her porcelain-white skin still haunt me. The ominous deadpan stare she wielded, with her teeth clenched in silent reprimand was an image etched into the psyche, never to be erased. Sister Earlene took a peculiar pleasure in public humiliation as a wicked tool. She orchestrated the classroom seating arrangement as a visible hierarchy of intellect, the brightest pupils occupied the front desks with each row marking a step down in academic esteem.

In this cruel tableau I found myself exiled to the very back, a testament to my holding the lowest grade point average in class. Predictably, I had to repeat the seventh grade. This academic failure only served as fodder for my father's scorn, providing him yet another pretext to underscore his perception of me as a *"dummy."*

The relentless critique and devaluation I endured were not just assaults on my intellectual capabilities but assaults on my very essence, chipping away at the brittle edifice of my self-worth.

Amidst this turmoil, there was one place where I found peace and could escape the brutality of my reality—the movie theater. It became my sanctuary, a place where for a few hours I could dive into stories of heroism and adventure, far from the cruelty I faced at home.

Sitting in front of the silver screen was a safe place where I could dream of a different life and flee from the grim realities of the world I inhabited. These moments in the dim light of the theater sowed the seeds of my Hollywood dreams. I envisioned myself growing up to be the leading man, capturing the love I yearned for but seldom got from my own family.

Despite the challenges I faced as a boy, these experiences shaped me into who I am. They fueled my determination to transform my life of shallow and despair into one of triumph. This dream wasn't just a fleeting thought; it was a beacon of hope, a goal firmly in my focus, inspired by the very challenges that tried to break me.

During my youth, I often found solace and a sense of belonging at the Boy's Club, spending a considerable amount of time away from home. Faced with the determination to overcome my vulnerable physique, I embarked on a disciplined journey at the age of twelve.

Each day I devoted myself to a rigorous exercise routine. Despite being a late bloomer, a significant growth spurt, combined with a commitment to weightlifting, boxing and martial arts, sculpted me into an extraordinary physical specimen.

When my family moved to Maryland for my father's new job at the Annapolis Naval Academy, I was enrolled into public school—and it was the best thing that could have ever happened to me. Unlike parochial school the public school system in Maryland provided art classes and a sports curriculum.

The stress relief I acquired from drawing, painting and sculpting, combined with physical education and competitive sports gave me refuge from the chaos of life at home. These activities allowed me to channel my energy and emotions into something constructive, creating a buffer against the world's pressures.

A boost in self-assurance fueled my freshman and sophomore years. I was longer the scrawny kid from Boston and my academic performance soared. I joined the Annapolis High School wrestling squad, and in my junior year, became the undefeated regional state champ.

The following year my father's government job put the family on the move again. This time to Subic Bay Naval Station in the Philippine Islands. I finished my senior year at Admiral George Dewey High School where I was the undefeated wrestling champion among all the American schools in the Philippines.

Before graduating high school in 1967, I received numerous wrestling scholarship offers, but the escalating Vietnam War called me into service. In September 1968,

Johnny Depp's Accidental Fixer

I enlisted in the U.S. Air Force. Following basic training, I served with the 636 Combat Support Group in Southeast Asia. I was later assigned to various bases in the U.S. and before receiving an honorable discharge in 1971, rose to the rank of Sergeant.

After transitioning to civilian life, I settled in Riverside, California, securing my first job managing a local gym. Shortly thereafter, fate had other plans for me. A chance encounter with a movie crew filming *'The Wild Party'* at the historic Mission Inn, in downtown Riverside, changed the course of my life.

Standing amidst the set's bustling activity, I was captivated by the enchantment of filmmaking—an art I had only ever observed from the audience's perspective. It was there at that moment that I was spotted by Ismail Merchant, the film's Academy Award-winning producer.

Paul Barresi

Nick Barresi *Miriam Barresi*

Annapolis High School Undefeated Wrestling Champion

Chapter 3
Hollywood's Hidden Truths

Ismail Merchant approached me, perhaps seeing something in me that I hadn't even recognized in myself. He offered me a job working behind the scenes during the filming of *'The Wild Party'* as a production assistant. More than just being given the opportunity to work as a PA, aka *"Go-For"* or *"Gopher"* in the Hollywood film world, it was a surreal moment for me. One minute I was an outsider looking in and the next, I was part of the very world that had offered me the escape I had longed for throughout my fractured childhood.

I would be tasked to do something as mundane as running errands for the film's star, 1960's Hollywood sex symbol Raquel Welch, or fetching a cup of coffee for the assistant director, or as involved as assisting the props man move heavy pieces of furniture on the set. It wasn't the most glamorous position working in the epitome of an entry-level position in the motion picture industry, but

I relished absorbing every bit I could about the process of filmmaking.

The watershed moment materialized when James Ivory, the film's director, who would later, the mastermind of Academy Award-nominated films, *'A Room with a View,' 'Howard's End,' 'The Remains of the Day'* and *'Call Me by Your Name'* extended to me my inaugural role in '*The Wild Party'* as the *bartender*. The opportunity to share the limelight in a musical sequence, with femme fatale Raquel Welch herself, transcended mere participation in a minor role; it ushered in the gritty reality of my childhood aspirations in the cinema's shadowed embrace.

An unexpected encounter unfolded when the art director of *Playgirl Magazine*, Robert Carpentier, visited the bustling movie set. After I finished my scene with Raquel, he approached me with an intriguing proposition to be *Playgirl's* the next centerfold. The newly founded American magazine was marketed primarily to women, featured nude and semi-nude men alongside general interest content, lifestyle pieces, celebrity journalism and original fiction.

I accepted Carpentier's offer which both flattered and surprised me, but it was the insight of *Playgirl's* iconic photographer, David Meyer, that redirected my path in a different, yet equally fascinating direction. He saw potential beyond the conventional, suggesting that my appearance would be more captivating if paired up with a beautiful woman.

Meyer's vision was avant-garde: a seven-page photo essay featuring a mortal man and woman, intergalactic lovers, adrift and entwined in the boundless expanse of outer space. This was not just any feature; it was a creative exploration of *Playgirl's* newly added erotic fantasy section- a venture that transcended beyond an ordinary modeling gig. It was a narrative of cosmic romance in a faraway galaxy.

The master lensman paired me up with his close friend, model and aspiring actress Cassandra Peterson, whose beauty was nothing short of stunning. Little did we know at the time, she would later soar to fame for her betrayal of the iconic horror hostess character *Elvira, 'Mistress of the Dark.'*

My futuristic photo layout in *Playgirl* with the future *Elvira*, was published in the March 1975. A blend of artistic vision and daring execution, the sellout issue proved to be a significant turning point, opening doors to surprising and unforeseen opportunities.

Andy Warhol framed the culture of the time, in his 1969 film, *'Blue Movie.'* This was the first adult erotic film depicting explicit sex to receive a wide theatrical release in the United States. According to Warhol, *'Blue Movie'* was a major influence in the making of *'Last Tango in Paris'* starring Marlon Brando. In 1970, *'The Devil in Miss Jones'* was one of the top ten most successful films of the year and was well-received by major media, including a favorable review by film critic Roger Ebert.

By the mid-1970s, newly won sexual freedoms were being exploited to capitalize on the increasingly open-minded society. Magazines depicting nudity, such as *Penthouse*, *Playboy*, and *Playgirl*, won acceptance as mainstream journals in which public figures felt safe expressing their fantasies. By the end of the 1980s, sexually explicit depictions were less stigmatized and more often seen in mainstream Hollywood films.

My featured appearance in *Playgirl* with Cassandra caught the eye of adult film producer Ted Paramore, who cast me in *'Co-ed Fever'* the first of dozens of erotic films in which I would appear. My aspirations stretched far beyond the confines of any single genre. Even as I continued to take on film roles with the *Playboy* channel and other leading producers of adult film entertainment, I never allowed my vision for a broader cinematic career to wane. While working in the adult entertainment industry, I continued to land speaking roles in mainstream Hollywood productions, including the film, *'Perfect,' 'Spontaneous Combustion,' and 'The Killing Jar'* as well as on television episodes like *'Father Dowling Mysteries'* and *Gabriel's Fire.'* I also toured the U.S. and Canada, performing on stage as Borden Eisler in the Neil Simon play, *'Plaza Suite'* starring *'Hollywood Squares'* and *'Bewitched'* comedic icon, Paul Lynde.

As a member of the Screen Actors Guild [SAG] in conjunction with my acting pursuits, I launched a parallel career into the realm of physical fitness, establishing my own sweat and slim enterprise, dedicated to personal workout regimens for Hollywood's elite. A pioneer of celebrity fitness training, I capitalized on my connections within Tinseltown to secure a clientele of luminaries such as record executive David Geffen, iconic playwright Neil Simon, late night king, Johnny Carson, *'Three's*

Company' star Joyce Dewitt, and comedic powerhouse, Joan Rivers.

A grim chapter in my multifaceted career unfolded in the predawn hours of January 11, 1982. Concerned for the welfare of my friend Paul Lynde who was conspicuously absent from my 33rd birthday celebration, I asked our mutual friend Dean Ditmann to accompany me to Paul's Beverly Hills home to check up on him.

Despite persistent knocking and ringing, Paul did not come to the door. His standard poodle, Alfred, barked wildly, adding to the urgency of the situation. Noticing the previous day's newspaper untouched on the doorstep heightened our concerns. As Dean anxiously looked on, I scaled the ten-foot iron carport gate.

Peering through the windows into the engulfing darkness, I heard only Alfred's distress calls. Our efforts to contact emergency services from a nearby payphone at Dan Tana's restaurant were fruitless, and the Beverly Hills police would not respond until 24 hours had passed.

With no other recourse, Dean and I returned to Paul's home. I forced my way through the side entrance, breaking glass, and splintering wood in the process, which set off the blaring house alarm. Upon entry, the unmistakable stench of death grew stronger, and Dean began to sob. Navigating through the pitch-black interior, guided by Alfred's incessant barking, and the shriek of the alarm, we found our way to the master bedroom. As we approached the bed, the stench of death grew stronger. The room was black. Dean cried aloud, repeatedly calling out Paul's name, and before I even turned on the lamp light, I knew he was gone.

Contrary to conspiracy theorists' dissemination of false rumors that Paul Lynde died due to nefarious circumstances, the coroner concluded after conducting an autopsy that he succumbed instantly to a massive heart attack.

My experience through the worlds of acting on stage, television, and in mainstream movies, in addition to sportwear modeling, and as a personal fitness trainer for the LaLa land elite, revealed the stark contrasts and contradictions of Hollywood. Initially drawn by the allure of cinematic success, I found myself navigating a path that led through the adult entertainment industry—a realm far removed from my childhood dreams.

This period of my life was not just about the roles I played on screen with or without the benefit of clothes, but a masterclass in understanding the multifaceted nature of fame and the delicate balance between public perception and personal integrity.

My odyssey in cinema began in the mainstream passageways of Hollywood, transitioned to the provocative realm of erotic film and return to the Hollywood mainstream. This trajectory illustrates that success can be achieved through a diverse array of paths fueled by ambition and a rich tapestry of real-life experiences that often find their reflection in the stories told on the silver screen.

The shift from personal fitness trainer to the stars to private investigation was more than a mere career change; it was a plunge into the mystic depths of the entertainment industry, a world I was already acquainted with. This transition was propelled by my growing disillusionment with Hollywood's superficial veneer, the pervasive casting couch scams, along with a burgeoning curiosity to uncover the clandestine narratives beneath its glamourous façade.

Fate seemed to guide my journey as I encountered industry insiders who recognized the value of my unique blend of insider knowledge and an outsider's perspective. It was during this phase that I crossed paths with Anthony Pellicano, a name synonymous with mystery and influence within Hollywood's secretive circles. During the ten years I conducted investigations under Pellicano's mentorship, I found myself at the center of countless Hollywood scandals and celebrity legal battles.

I attribute my refined observational acumen and innate investigative skills to the formative years of my upbringing. Navigating a turbulent childhood within a household of turmoil where the omnipresent specter of physical and emotional peril loomed large, honed my skills remarkably, preparing me for a career in private investigation. This chaotic environment cultivated an innate ability within me to detect when individuals were concealing truths. It enhanced my capacity to identify and monitor threats, as well as to recall adverse events with striking clarity.

The unpredictability of my upbringing has rendered me more adept at task shifting, particularly in scenarios that echo elements of my childhood experiences. Delving into the Depp v. Heard saga seemed almost predestined for me. Early into my investigation, I found the parallels between the tumult of my youth and the experiences Johnny Depp encountered in his early life remarkably striking.

As Pellicano's trusted confidant for more than a decade, I navigated the murky waters of the decadent underworld, helping to quash career-damaging, sexually based scandals for a plethora of high-profile clients, including athletes, record moguls, business executives, politicians, and Hollywood megastars. My association with the *"fixer of fixers"* took a dramatic turn in 2002 when a federal investigation into his activities unfolded.

The subsequent FBI raid on Pellicano's offices uncovered a trove of incriminating evidence, including two modified hand grenades designed to function as homemade bombs, military-grade C-4 plastic explosives. A vast quantity of computer files was seized, becoming the focus of a sweeping federal grand jury investigation into allegations of illegal wiretappings conducted by my former boss on behalf of the prominent Hollywood attorneys who hired him.

This led to a sweeping federal grand jury probe, and subsequently, my mentor, who I endearingly hailed as the *"fissatore di fissatori"* was charged with possession of unregistered firearms, plastic explosives, and unlawful storage of explosive materials. His guilty plea and subsequent thirty-month federal prison sentence marked the end of an era and a pivotal turning point in my journey, propelling me into a new chapter of my own story. In the sultry summer of 2004, my past entanglements with Pellicano, thrust me into the FBI's spotlight. On August 4th, a call from Special Agent Stan Ornellas pierced the tranquility of my day, beckoning me to a clandestine meeting. We set a date for the following week at Giorgio's, an Italian restaurant in Studio City.

Arriving with the punctuality of a seasoned operative, I chose a strategic position near the window, looking out into the parking lot, a perfect vantage point to assess my soon-to-be interrogators. Ornellas, a colossus of a man, exuded an aura of formidable strength, a stark contrast to his partner, Special Agent Tom Ballard, whose lanky frame, and pale demeanor suggested a predilection for the cerebral rather than the physical.

The air was thick with tension. As we convened at the table, the special agents' reluctance to engage in pleasantries or even partake in the culinary offerings told me this was going to be a bumpy ride. Signaling the gravity of the matter at hand, the duo wasted no time delving into the crux of their interest: what I knew about Aikido instructor turned actor Steven Seagal.

This intense scrutiny was precipitated by the FBI raid on Pellicano's offices, initiated after Los Angeles Times reporter Anita Busch, investigating a suspected collusion with Seagal and an Italian mob figure, found a dead fish with a rose in its mouth and a menacing note on her car windshield. The FBI initially suspected Seagal was behind the traumatic threat on Busch.

I confided to the special agents that in 2002, after Hollywood film maker Jules Nasso filed a $60 million lawsuit against Seagal for abandoning a four-picture deal, he recruited my investigative services against the action star. Nasso, who had been instrumental in catapulting Seagal to stardom with movies like, *'Marked for Death,' 'Out for Justice,' 'Above the Law,"* and *'Under Siege,'* felt deeply betrayed. He alleged that Seagal, a former friend and business partner, was the orchestrator of the attack on Los Angeles Times reporter Anita Busch, due to a long-standing animosity towards reporters, particularly female journalists. Driven to undermine Seagal's reputation, the acclaimed producer retained my services to substantiate these claims.

Ornellas and Ballard initially doubted the feasibility of this mission until I shared harrowing details of how I acquired a raw, unedited 1988 audio interview of Seagal with *Gallery Magazine*, conducted after the release of the release of *'Above the Law.'* In the revealing two-hour session, *Gallery's* columnist, Bob Ellison, probes the action star about any perceived differences between men and women interviewers. Seagal candidly responds, *"Well, interesting enough, the few times that I had a hard time it was usually with women."* He vividly recalls one incident with palpable disdain: *"One time, it was just some dumb cunt,"* who led him to conclude she was soliciting a romantic involvement, only to rebuff his advances.

Speaking in the collective, he vehemently continues, *"They're a bunch of dirty fucking whores who belong in a zoo,"* and harshly criticizes their professional choices, stating, *"They should not have chosen journalism as a profession, they should be working in porn, or something like that."* I told the agents that this was part of a broader, toxic pattern reflecting a grim reality of the industry, where the affluent and influential movers and shakers in Hollywood often manipulate and degrade women.

Steven Seagal was eventually cleared, but more than two decades later, the paunchy former action star is still waiting for an apology from the feds for their criminal allegations and his public humiliation.

The special agents' queries then centered on the lawyers who engaged Pellicano's services. They expressed a particular interest in Tom Cruise's general counsel Bert Fields, and his divorce lawyer Dennis Wasser. This query was understandable because during the raid on Pellicano's office, the FBI also uncovered wiretapped telephone conversations following the 2001 announcement about Cruise's divorce with Nicole Kidman.

Divulging my involvement in the more obscure aspects of the *'Eyes Wide Shut'* star's divorce from his co-star, I confided to the agents that while the couple were negotiating a divorce settlement, Pellicano tasked me to assist him in silencing a male prostitute who alleged an illicit liaison with Cruise during his marriage to Kidman.

I told the agents that I successfully located the street hustler, *Nathan*, in a dingy, West Hollywood bar, and successfully helped him see his way clear to stop spreading lies. After the dirty work was done, Bert Fields fired off a cease-and-desist letter to him, after which, he vehemently denied ever having an intimate relationship with Cruise and was never heard from again.

Even though their work on behalf of the *'Mission Impossible – Dead Reckoning'* star was successful, there was little celebration. Fields was under federal investigation and Wasser became a person of interest. Fortunately, both of Cruise's legal representatives were eventually exonerated of any wrongdoing.

As for Anthony Pellicano, the ordeal was far from over. On February 3, 2006, only one day before his scheduled release from prison, he was arrested again and charged with 110 counts, including illegal wiretapping, bribery, racketeering, conspiracy, witness tampering, identity theft, and destruction of evidence. Specifically, he was accused of unlawfully obtaining confidential records on celebrities and public figures from members of the Los Angeles and Beverly Hills police departments. Pellicano remained in prison until March 22, 2019.

Reflecting on my transition from actor to Hollywood sleuth, I see it not as a departure from the entertainment industry but as an evolution. From the mean streets of Boston to the underbelly of Hollywood, where appearances often mask a different reality, I've come to appreciate the value of resilience.

My story, intertwined with the narratives I sought to uncover, is a testament to the power of perseverance and the importance of seeking truth. This journey has been more than just a career; it has been a profound exploration of the hidden narratives that shape our perceptions and our lives.

As I stood on the cusp of delving into the investigation's core, with the preliminary strategies unfolding before me, I felt the profound weight of responsibility that this role entailed. This endeavor extended beyond professional boundaries; it was a natural progression of my lifelong pursuit to uncover truth amidst obscurity and to illuminate the intricacies that shape our existence. With each step planned and each strategic discussion that molded my path forward, my awareness of the impending challenges grew.

Venturing into uncharted territories, I was fortified by the lessons gleaned from my past experiences and poised to uncover a narrative in Depp v. Heard that had seized the global imagination. I was ready to embark on this journey and fully prepared to navigate through the maze of celebrity and scandal, driven by an unwavering resolve to uncover the truths veiled within.

Johnny Depp's Accidental Fixer

The Wild Party with Raquel Welch

1970's erotic film star

Chapter 4
The Hunt Begins

As dawn broke, the real work commenced. The first day of the investigation was marked by a flurry of activity. I convened with my database expert early in the morning. The air was thick with anticipation; we were about to delve into the unknown. I laid out the framework of the investigation, identifying key players, potential witnesses, and avenues for gathering evidence. While scouring social media and public records for clues, I readied myself for doing the fieldwork, conducting interviews and surveillance.

My second meeting with Amber's lawyers Rick Schwartz and Eric George also took place amidst the opulence of Brown George Ross LLP's offices, a setting that could easily distract one with its panoramic views of the California coastline. Yet, the gravity of our conversation anchored us firmly to the matter at hand. They laid out the blueprint of our quest, reiterating for emphasis and clarity, the weight that tangible evidence of violence, especially photographic or video proof, would hold. The stakes were clear, as well as their belief in my abilities to unearth the evidence needed to corroborate Amber's allegations.

Getting down to the real work at hand, my suggestion to approach former adult film star turned mainstream Hollywood actress Traci Lords, about her experiences with Johnny during the making of *'Cry- Baby,'* was met with an immediate and enthusiastic endorsement from Eric George.

His words, *"It's time for someone to speak up and call out Johnny for his phony bullshit claim to be as nonviolent as Gandhi,"* resonated with a mix of resolve and the anticipation of challenges to come.

The consensus was clear: eyewitness testimony or documented proof of Johnny's alleged violent behavior was essential, yet the path to finding willing witnesses was fraught with hurdles, not least the fear of career repercussions.

In the realm of this world, especially Hollywood, where every step is scrutinized, casting someone into the heart of an unwelcome scandal inevitably casts a shadow over one's own reputation. This truth underscores the importance of maintaining bridges in the enigmatic world of Hollywood, where severing connections can spell the end of a career. The adage, *"You'll never work in this town again,"* is a testament to this reality.

———⚖———

Efforts to engage Traci whom incidentally, I appeared with in *'Miss Passion'* five years before she was featured with Johnny in *'Cry-Baby'* proved futile. Despite this, I managed to connect with someone close to the situation, Traci's friend *Lisa*.

Lisa shared insights into Traci's interactions with Johnny, diverging from the speculative rumors of a sexual relationship during their filming together. According to *Lisa,* Traci's recollections of Johnny were nothing but positive. She esteemed him as *"a genuine southern gentleman,"*—a portrayal that stood in stark contrast to the depiction offered by Amber's lawyer Eric George in *People Magazine,* in which he stated, *"The evidence in this case [Depp v. Heard] is clear: Johnny Depp repeatedly beat Amber Heard."* George continued, *"The increasingly desperate attempts by Mr. Depp and his enablers to revive his career by initiating baseless litigation against so many people once close to him — his former lawyers, former managers, and his former spouse — are not fooling anyone."*

Johnny Depp's Accidental Fixer

The investigation's complexity intensified with George's comments, painting Johnny in a light far removed from the shy, unassuming character that *Lisa* depicted based on her discussions about Johnny's interactions with Traci. This contrast between public declarations and private perceptions highlighted the convoluted nature of unraveling the truth amidst Hollywood's glittering facades.

As I maneuvered through the congested streets of Los Angeles, my mind raced, piecing together a strategy from the fragments of information and speculation that had been shared with me. My home office became the epicenter of an exhaustive search through the digital and social fabrics connecting Johnny to the world. Contact information for anyone remotely linked to him was gathered with meticulous care, setting the stage for a series of interviews that I hoped would uncover deeper truths about his public persona.

The night wore on and as I delved into the allegations shared by Amber, and her dynamic legal eagles, I found myself questioning the narrative that had been painted. Based on the dozens and dozens of media reports I examined objectively, I found that Johnny is portrayed more as a reveler than a perpetrator of violence. And this put me at odds with the mission I had been tasked with.

As the investigation deepened, my nights became a blend of determination and relentless pursuit, each piece of evidence a potential key to the truth. A story from the *Daily Mail UK* that Rick Schwartz Esq. forwarded to me recounted an incident that allegedly occurred in the early morning hours of June 2, 2016, involving Johnny Depp and his bodyguards outside a casino in Denmark following a late-night celebration.

The headline itself was a mouthful which read, *"Johnny Depp in 2 a.m. Altercation with Bodyguards Outside Casino After Swinging Champagne at Concert After Party in Denmark... and Flirting with a Mystery Blonde,"* hinted at a brute force scenario. Yet, once again, after combing through the details, fairly and objectively, I concluded that the story illustrated a night of excess rather than outright violence.

Johnny had been reveling with his band, The Hollywood Vampires, a group graced by the likes of Alice Cooper and Joe Perry. The narrative depicted a scene of celebration turned chaotic, with Johnny at the center, resisting attempts by his bodyguard to bring the night to a close. A brunette woman's efforts to console him painted a picture of a man caught in a moment of defiance, fueled by alcohol, yet the narrative was peppered with uncertainty, the word "apparently" casting doubt on the solidity of the account.

This portrayal clashed with the mission at hand to uncover evidence of Johnny's alleged propensity to violence. Instead, the article offered a glimpse into a world of celebrity excess, and living it up, where the lines between boisterous, drunken celebration and physical aggression seemed blurred. It was a reminder of the challenges that lay ahead in distinguishing the man from the myth, the truth from the tabloid. Yet, this was but one piece of the puzzle, a snapshot of a larger, more complex picture that I was determined to piece together.

The investigation took a pivotal turn on July 10, 2019, when Schwartz introduced several new pieces of evidence for my examination. Among these was a captivating email exchange between himself and Amber Heard's then-public relations experts. The conversation revolved around a request for proof of Johnny's alleged cocaine use, which led to the presentation of a Vimeo video. This video showcased a conspicuous white stain on Johnny's jacket during a European film premiere—an image they implied was incriminating. Wishful thinking stands in the way of reality. To my mind there was an equal possibility the substance could have been as innocuous as a piece of cheesecake, perhaps accidentally dropped from his fork, or bird droppings for that matter.

The leap to conclude that this stain was indicative of cocaine use struck me as a significant overreach, a departure from tangible evidence into the realm of speculation. This instance was not about identifying a definitive proof but rather observing a moment where reality was stretched thin by imagination.

The eagerness of Amber's PR team to infer drug abuse from such a circumstantial detail highlighted a tendency to favor sensationalism over fact. There is a public perception that PR people tend to reach for straws in defense of their beloved clients, but in my profession, we reach for facts. Relying solely on such assumptions can lead investigators astray.

My role is not to gather hopeful interpretations but to seek out undeniable truths. In the complex web of Hollywood narratives, discerning the truth requires more than quantum leaps—it demands rigorous evidence and a commitment to reality.

Johnny Depp's Accidental Fixer

An August 12, 2016, *TMZ* exclusive titled *"Johnny Depp Goes Off on Amber H.,"* I was tasked to examine what was purported to have been filmed before the May 21, 2016, incident where Amber alleged Johnny struck her. The stakes were high. I was told that the video's contents had the potential to significantly impact public perception favorable to Amber.

In the video, Amber is seen trying to calm Johnny down, asking if he drank a whole bottle of wine. Although Amber apologizes for an unspecified reason, I found the context to be nebulous and shrouded in ambiguity.

Sources close to Johnny asserted that the video was *"heavily edited,"* suggesting Amber was seen smiling and provoking Johnny, thereby casting more doubt on the narrative of him as the aggressor. Some claimed it was a setup by Amber, designed to create physical evidence supporting her narrative of seeking to help Johnny in his impaired state.

After reviewing the video numerous times, it became evident that Johnny was aware of Amber's intentions, as he attempted, although unsuccessfully, to snatch her phone. This act, in the eyes of some, could be seen as a natural response to being recorded without consent, especially in a vulnerable state.

Despite the contentious nature of the graphical footage and the claims of manipulation, my analysis led me to conclude that if admitted as evidence, the video might favor Johnny rather than Amber. The episode appeared scripted, on Amber's part, and came off as phony altruism that I just could not buy. Coming from a movie buff for as long as I can remember, had I watched the ghastly scene unfold on the silver screen, I would have walked out.

The layers of interpretation surrounding the video underscored the complex dynamics at play, revealing a saga of love, turmoil, and the quest for truth amidst the spectacle of celebrity. The video incident served yet another stark reminder of the challenges inherent in discerning fact from fiction. The narrative constructed by the video was contentious, laden with accusations and counteraccusations that painted a picture of a relationship fraught with tension and misunderstanding.

This stage of my investigation was emblematic of the broader struggle to navigate the murky waters of high-profile legal battles, where evidence is not merely a matter of fact but a battleground for competing narratives.

The ramifications of the escapade caught on tape extended beyond the immediate legal implications, casting a veil of shadow over the public discourse surrounding Johnny and Amber's tempestuous relationship. It was a testament to the power of media in shaping perceptions and the precarious balance between privacy and public interest.

With each step into the investigation, clarity waned as I navigated a labyrinth of narratives, each offering a distinct lens through which to view Johnny Depp. The wide variety of intelligence provided by Schwartz served as guideposts, directing me down divergent paths in search of elusive truths about Depp's character. Doubt was my constant companion as I scrutinized accounts that portrayed Johnny in a light starkly different from the violent image under scrutiny.

It was imperative to adopt a critical mindset, scrutinizing each piece of evidence and its significance to the broader investigation. This meticulous process was vital in attempting to construct a cohesive narrative from the myriad of stories, rumors, and testimonies surrounding Depp's contentious persona. Each narrative thread contributed another layer to the intricate tapestry that constitutes Johnny Depp's public and private existence, rendering the quest for truth as challenging as it was enthralling.

Kyra Kramer's piece, *"Johnny Depp's History of Violence"* was one such breadcrumb that initially promised a feast of facts but instead offered a platter of suppositions. Her attempt to juxtapose Johnny with figures marred by accusations of violence and misconduct was an intriguing narrative strategy, yet it was the reliance on tentative language—*"seems to be," "obviously is,"*—that raised flags for me. These expressions, peppered throughout the article, signaled a foundation built on assumption rather than concrete evidence.

It became increasingly apparent that Kramer's perspective was profoundly influenced by her alignment with the Me-Too movement—a commendable cause, but her deep emotional investment seemed to obscure her ability to impartially evaluate Johnny's actions. Her article portrayed Amber as a symbol of gender justice, akin to a contemporary Joan of Arc from the ACLU, who courageously led the battle for freedom during the Hundred Years War against England.

Defying tremendous odds, just as the French national heroine found herself overwhelmed by the Burgundian forces, Amber found herself besieged by an intense onslaught from ardent supporters of Captain Jack Sparrow. Tragically mirroring history, like *Jeanne di' Arc*, faced brutal execution at the stake in the French city of Rouen, Amber would also endure a bloodthirsty, public execution of her character, in Fairfax County, Virginia.

As I progressed in my investigation, the insights gained from this endeavor remained ingrained in my consciousness, serving as a perpetual reminder of the complexity of human relationships and the evasive nature of truth under the intense scrutiny of the public eye.

Chapter 5
The Viper Room History

My task was formidable: to explore the ominous *"Dark Shadows"* in Johnny Depp's history, searching for evidence of violent tendencies that might support Amber Heard's accusations against him. My investigation would lead me from the glitzy streets of Hollywood—where the entertainment elite gathered to revel and be seen in nightclubs, rock venues, bars, diners, comedy halls, and eateries—to the more secluded, personal realms of those who had once been close to Depp.

In a tension-filled conference room, where the air hung heavy with expectancy, I presented my proposal for an extensive inquiry into Depp's history. I emphasized the necessity of recognizing that manifestations of anger do not emerge in isolation; they are frequently entrenched in one's formative years. *"Rage begins in childhood"* I pondered aloud, proposing a journey back to 1993. That year, Hollywood's golden boy had already attained the pinnacle of international fame with box-

Johnny Depp's Accidental Fixer

office hits like *'Edward Scissorhands,' 'Freddy's Dead: The Final Nightmare'* and *'What's Eating Gilbert Grape.'* It was also the year Depp inaugurated The Viper Room, a notorious nightclub on the Sunset Strip. I believed that within this venue, amidst the remnants of Hollywood's more tumultuous periods, I would uncover the initial strands of the narrative I sought to piece together.

This line of reasoning gained the approval of Eric George, Esq. but not Rick Schwartz, Esq. *"I'll need Amber's approval for this,"* Schwartz cautioned, his tone somber. *"I doubt she'll go along with the idea, but I'll ask her."* Later, upon returning to my residence, I received a notification—an email from Schwartz: *"I just heard back from Amber, and she agrees that investigating Johnny's past is a good idea, so, since her wish is my command, happy hunting."*

A surge of relief swept through me—Amber's consent was crucial. I now had the green light to delve deeper into the enigmatic past of Johnny Depp during his younger years. He was known for his lavish spending and hedonistic lifestyle, potentially marked by a lack of accountability or commitment. I speculated that if there were ever a time when Depp might have lost control and physically assaulted someone, it would be during this era of unrestrained social life where anything seemed permissible. I embarked on a mission to investigate Depp's past, focusing on the tangled history of the Viper Room, the nightclub he purchased in 1993 that soon became synonymous with Hollywood nightlife.

Originally opened by Anthony Fox as The Central, a somewhat nondescript bar lacking glamour or intrigue, Depp cleverly circumvented the bureaucratic hurdles that often-hindered liquor licensing by forming a partnership with Fox. This marked the beginning of the Viper Room's rise to fame. The nightclub's notoriety peaked only months later when tragically, on Halloween night, actor River Phoenix, one of the brightest young stars of his generation, collapsed and died of a drug overdose right outside the club's doors. The incident cast a long, dark shadow over the Viper Room, and it became a place forever linked to the dangers of excess in the celebrity world.

Digging deeper into the nightclub's history revealed a complex web of ambition, mystery, and conflict. Anthony Fox, who held 49% ownership, had been instrumental in helping Johnny get the club up and running, found himself embroiled in a bitter legal battle with Depp over financial discrepancies. He accused Depp of sidelining him financially, a dispute that was poised to come to a head in court.

In January 2000, just days before Fox was scheduled to testify against Depp and other co-defendants, alleging financial fraud, he mysteriously disappeared. Just before Christmas, on December 19, 2001, his pick-up truck was found abandoned.

The Ventura Police Department opened a missing persons investigation. Fox's sudden and unexplained disappearance fueled endless speculation and dark rumors about the nature of his relationship with Depp and whether his disappearance was connected to their impending legal clash.

The ongoing mystery of Fox's disappearance added a sinister layer to the Viper Room's story, intertwining it irrevocably with tales of betrayal and loss. The club continued to operate, its every corner echoing with the ghosts of its tumultuous past, a past that I was now trying to piece together.

Each person I spoke with that missing persons detectives didn't question; each document I unearthed that missing person's detectives had no knowledge of, brought me closer to the circumstances surrounding

Depp's former business partner's sudden disappearance. My investigation demanded a careful sifting through rumors and hearsay to unearth the facts. The Viper Room with its storied history of glory and tragedy, held the keys to many secrets and I was determined to uncover them.

There was a mystery about the story. Johnny Depp, international movie star and his missing business partner. Was it murder? Was it suicide? There was no lack of conspiracy theories. Delving deeper into the mystery, my journey took a pivotal turn when I interviewed Anthony Fox's ex-wife, Judy Mcbane. She was a wellspring of untold stories, revealing a startling encounter with her ex-husband, whom she called "Tony," six months after he had allegedly vanished. Her narrative was captivating.

Judy recounted, *"I spotted Tony at a Barnes & Noble in Montclair, California, in mid-June 2002. I was searching for the Red Rose series, and there he was, right beside me, engrossed in a book."* Her conviction in recognizing her ex-husband was unwavering, a confidence born from over a decade of shared memories and intimate familiarity: She explained, *"I was married to the man for seven years. He was in his usual attire – a*

T-shirt and jeans, and that bald head and prominent nose of his are unmistakable."

Judy's alleged brief exchange with Tony was fraught with tension, a fleeting glance that spoke volumes before he hastily retreated. Judy attempted to follow but lost him amidst the bustling streets. Nevertheless, she managed to note the license plate of the white Honda he drove off in. Despite her efforts and subsequent reporting to the Ventura Police Department, the information led nowhere, engulfing Judy in years of silence and speculation over her former spouse's potential orchestration of his own disappearance.

The backdrop of their stormy relationship painted a picture rich with financial deceit, emotional turmoil and a fractured family dynamic. Judy revealed Tony's longstanding obsession with wealth and his dual citizenship in the US and UK, hinting at motives behind what she characterized as his *"vanishing act."*

Shedding light on the deep financial roots that may have influenced her ex-husband's actions, Judy whispered, *"Tony's mother Maud once told us she was so wealthy she didn't know how much money she had."* An old letter from Tony just days following their separation in March 1995 hinted at a premeditated plan to return to

England if he could not find work. Several weeks after receiving the letter, Judy went to his apartment to find his living quarters in disarray, a scene she believed was staged for effect. Judy recounted how she *"tracked Tony down, living with his so-called girlfriend,"* and confronted him about his *"vanishing act." "Why did you disappear,"* to which Tony barked, *"Because I wanted to get rid of you!"*

Tony's financial manipulations extended to his stake in the Viper Room, with Judy questioning the veracity of his claims about the club's finances. The mystery deepened with her insights into their personal life, marked by financial exploitation and emotional abuse.

Judy's narrative offered a glimpse into a life upended by Tony's schemes, from a once-content existence to a reality marred by deceit and hardship. Her reflections on her ex-husband's partnership with Johnny Depp and the possible motivations behind it added another puzzle piece to his disappearance.

This exploration into the enigma of Anthony Fox's disappearance, guided by Judy's poignant recollections, unveiled a labyrinth of potential leads and motivations. It was clear that the journey to uncover the truth was far from over, promising further revelations in this intricate saga.

Intrigued by the substantial wealth of Anthony Fox's lineage, I deepened my examination of his distinguished family. An official document from the 1911 Census of England & Wales revealed that Fox's grandfather, Dr. Wilfred Fox, was not only a decorated World War I British military officer but also a man of considerable affluence and influence. He received the prestigious Victoria Medal of Honor and even served as an advisor to King George V on the royal gardens.

My research uncovered that in May 1952, Anthony Fox's grandfather donated 62 acres, including the upper lake, to the National Trust. This act of generosity established what is known today as Winkworth Arboretum.

Anthony's father, Vivian, amassed significant wealth as the owner and operator of silver mines in Peru, South America. He and his wife, Maud, raised their sons, Anthony, and his older brother, Charles, in the UK. Upon retiring, they relocated to Onslow Square in South Kensington, London.

After Anthony's father's death in 1976, he left his family financially secure, ensuring that the legacy of prosperity and influence would continue.

This lineage of affluence and significant contributions to society painted a complex picture of the Fox family. From the establishment of Winkworth Arboretum to the wealth generated from South American silver mines, the Fox family history is one of remarkable generosity and entrepreneurial success. These revelations provided a deeper understanding of Anthony Fox's background, linking his life to a heritage of both social prominence and altruistic endeavors.

I discussed Anthony's lawsuit against Johnny with Los Angeles attorney Allison Hart, who represented one of the co-defendants in the case. Contrary to some media reports and conspiracy theories suggesting Depp's involvement in Fox's disappearance, Hart confided, *"At the time of his disappearance, Fox was on the losing side in court."* The exceptional lawyer with extensive experience litigating cases before state and federal courts added, *"He had little chance of prevailing."* While Hart's statement reduced the probability of Depp's involvement in his former business partner's disappearance, my commitment to uncovering the

Johnny Depp's Accidental Fixer

unequivocal truth intensified, rather than simply gathering evidence to incriminate the famed actor.

My journey continued at the Superior Court archives in downtown Los Angeles, where I was greeted by several crates brimming with documents and multiple exhibits from the legal battle between Anthony Fox and Johnny Depp. The daunting volume of paperwork would have taken an eternity to sift through. To save time, I asked the clerk to provide me with the most pertinent files for my investigation.

Within these legal filings I discovered validation for Ms. Hart's assertions. Fox's determination was palpable as he frequently returned to court, doggedly seeking a different verdict. A specific ruling caught my attention—DBA, The Viper, Case No: SS008992—where the presiding judge noted that despite two previous attempts, Fox had violated the California Code of Civil Procedure by filing a third appeal without presenting new evidence or legal grounds. The judge reprimanded and fined him for this frivolous action.

The more I delved into the case, the clearer it became that Fox's legal strategy was increasingly desperate. His repeated attempts to overturn prior rulings highlighted a man grasping at straws, trying to reclaim what he believed was rightfully his. These findings painted a picture of a legal battle fraught with frustration and diminishing hope for Fox. Despite the overwhelming odds against him, Fox's persistence was evident, yet it seemed to underscore the futility of his efforts rather than any genuine prospect of success.

As I pieced together the narrative from these documents, the complexities of the case became more apparent. The legal wrangling, marked by numerous appeals and mounting tensions, provided a stark contrast to the sensationalized stories circulating in the media. This deeper understanding of the legal proceedings, combined with the insights from the accredited lawyer Allison Hart, shifted the focus of my investigation towards a more nuanced exploration of the circumstances surrounding Fox's disappearance. My goal was no longer simply to find evidence but to construct a comprehensive picture of the truth, free from the distortions of rumor and speculation.

The Honorable Valerie Baker, who presided over the case, stated in her Memorandum of Points and Authorities: *"Not satisfied at having had two bites of the apple, Petitioner Anthony Fox has brought a motion for reconsideration in the hopes of obtaining a third."* The

Judge went on to state, *"For wasting the Court's and Respondent's* [Johnny Depp's] *time and resources in bringing his wholly improper motion, Petitioner* [Anthony Fox] *should be sanctioned in the amount of $1,800.00."*

Vital statistics records from the Wandsworth District of London revealed that Anthony's mother, Maud Rebecca Fox, passed away in March 2004. Intriguingly, also in 2004, Johnny Depp transferred his share of the Viper Room to Anthony's daughter, Constance Amanda Fox.

Examining Maud's Last Will and Testament became a priority, as it potentially held the key to understanding the financial and familial dynamics at play. This document could reveal whether Anthony's actions were driven by financial desperation, a strategic maneuver to secure his legacy, or something even more complex.

The more I unearthed, the more I realized that each layer of this story required scrutiny. The legal battles, the family inheritance, and the shifting ownership of significant assets all pointed to a narrative far richer and more convoluted than initially apparent. My goal was to piece together these elements to form a coherent and truthful account of what transpired, shining a light on the factors that might have contributed to Anthony Fox's abrupt disappearance.

I procured a copy of the Will that Anthony Fox's mother Maud had curiously modified shortly after her son's disappearance. It uncovered pivotal clues, including the names of significant individuals whom Ventura Police detectives, despite two decades of inquiry, had failed to question.

I decided to pursue these clues on my own. The surprising facts revealed in Maud's Will were astounding. She specified that if her son Anthony was not found within two years following her death, then his share of the inheritance would be divided equally between his older brother Charles and his daughter Constance Amanda Fox. I discovered that two years following Maud's death in March 2004, Anthony's brother Charles received his half—a substantial sum, while his daughter Constance did not.

The overlooked details in Maud's Will and the subsequent handling of the inheritance, provided critical insights into the Fox family's financial dynamics. It also highlighted significant lapses in the investigation conducted by the missing persons detectives of the Ventura Police Department.

Determined to see justice served, I contacted Constance and encourage her to pursue her rightful claim. During my interview with her she revealed crucial evidence overlooked by the missing persons detectives. Constance told me that she was still a minor and residing with her father when he disappeared. She recounted tearfully: *"I was rushed out of our apartment and placed into protective custody so fast, I didn't have enough time to pack all my things. I wasn't even allowed to check the answering machine! What if my father had called!"*

The most striking revelation came to light when I interviewed Anthony Fox's older brother Charles in Somerset England. He shared a startling disclosure: *"Just before Christmas before Tony disappeared, my mother had received a letter from Tony."*

It typically takes four to seven days for a letter to arrive in the UK from California. Given that Maud received the letter *"just before Christmas,"* I surmised that Anthony mailed it on or about December 19, 2001, the very day his pickup truck was found abandoned.

Charles recounted, *"I asked my mother to tell me what was in the letter, but she refused. After she died, when I was packing up her things, I searched everywhere for the letter but found no trace of it. She took it to her grave I'm afraid, which is unfortunate because therein, the mystery of my brother's disappearance resides."*

Detective Anthony Reginato with the missing persons division of the Ventura Police Department acknowledged that before I provided detectives with the new information, they were no closer to solving the case than they were when Fox disappeared more than two decades ago. Reginato was clear, *"Contrary to all the crazy conspiracy theories, Johnny has never been a suspect in his former business partner's mysterious disappearance."*

I closed this phase of my investigation, concluding that the circumstances surrounding Anthony Fox's disappearance suggests a possible cover-up.

Aware that pursuing interviews with former patrons, employees, associates, and musicians who came and went at the Viper Room would illuminate aspects of Depp's other entanglements with the nightclub, my primary challenge was identifying these individuals and then figuring out how to reach them. Tracking down these key witnesses required meticulous research and a network of contacts willing to provide leads. Each interview had the potential to reveal critical insights,

Johnny Depp's Accidental Fixer

helping to piece together a clearer picture of Depp's role in the nightclub's history.

During my research, I discovered that former child actress Olivia Barash worked at the Viper Room. Her acting career started with appearances in television series like *'Little House on the Prairie,' 'Charlie's Angels,'* and later secured supporting roles in films such as *'Repo Man,' 'Tuff Turf,' 'Patty Hearst,'* and *'Floundering.'* I located her through standard database channels, and she graciously agreed to an interview.

Olivia confided that she was producing a documentary titled *'Friends of the Viper Room,'* when the venue hosted bands like The Wallflowers, The Pussycat Dolls, Counting Crows, and The Black-Eyed Peas on their ascent to fame. Unfortunately, her project had stalled due to fundraising difficulties.

Olivia described her relationship with Depp during her time working at the club as a programmer in the 1990s. *"Johnny was sweet and gentle—a truly kind man,"* she remarked, insisting, *"I have never seen him be violent toward anyone."* Olivia impressed me as an earnest and candid individual. She emphatically stated, *"Johnny doesn't have a mean bone in his body."* Through she provided no information that Amber would find useful, she did offer me the names of several people from her days at the Viper Room—former patrons, employees, performers and the like, which I greatly appreciated.

Unbeknownst to me at the time of our interview, Olivia's positive recollections of Depp and her characterization of him would echo a consistent theme that I encountered in dozens of interviews I conducted to follow. Presenting all the testimonials would require multiple volumes. A selected few are worth sharing, starting with my interview with Richmond Arquette, of the Arquette acting clan.

Now a successful actor, writer and producer with notable roles in films like *'Zodiac,' 'Fight Club,' 'Pulp Fiction,'* and *'The People vs. Larry Flynt'* the former barback who worked at the Viper Room from 1994 to 1996, branded Depp, *"A gentleman's gentleman."* During our one-hour interview, he assured me that he never witnessed Depp display any violence. *"I've always known Johnny to be an even-tempered guy who treated people with kindness."* Richmond emphasized that despite many women pursuing him, often aggressively, he remained gracious and respectful. *"Johnny was a great boss and paid well."* He fondly recalled being introduced to Depp's then-girlfriend, Kate Moss at the

Viper Room, concluding, *"I have nothing but good memories of Johnny and my time working there."*

I conducted another comprehensive interview with actress, producer and award-winning journalist Seven McDonald, who managed the Viper Room from 1994 to early 1996. With a journalism background including stints at *Harper's Bazaar*, *Nylon*, and *Playboy*, she also boasts an extensive film, TV, and music industry résumé. As a young actress, Seven was a semi-regular on Norman Lear's *'Archie Bunker's Place.'* She revealed that she and Johnny had been acquaintances since their teenage years and expressed enduring affection for him, stating, *"I will always love him."* When I first contacted Seven and mentioned my work was for Amber, she hesitated, remarking, *"I don't think I can help you. Johnny is a sweet man. I've never seen him be violent—in fact, just the opposite,"* she added, *"Johnny Depp is the type who would crawl down a drainpipe to save a kitten from drowning."*

Iconic songwriter, musician and one of Depp's closest of friends, Chuck Weiss, passed away nearly two years after my interview with him. Weiss and his band, The Goddamn Liars, played occasionally at the Viper Room. A Denver native, he was a dedicated musicologist, known for his encyclopedic knowledge of obscure jazz and early R&B artists. His debut album, *'The Other Side of Town'* was released in 1981, and years later he produced *'Extremely Cool'* with Johnny as the executive producer. Their shared passion for music led them to collaborate on opening the Viper Room.

After several unsuccessful attempts to reach Weiss, I did what any private dick would do when all else failed—I door-stepped him. When I appeared at his doorstep, he was laid back on the front porch, strumming his guitar. He told me right off the bat that he had already been forewarned I'd likely be showing up uninvited, but he greeted me with a warm hello, nonetheless.

Weiss agreed to afford me gave me a moment of his time because, as he so poetically put it, telling me what an exceptional human being Johnny Depp is was nothing to hide. Weiss stated that he and Johnny have known each other for years. *"Nobody knows what goes on behind closed doors, but in my presence, Johnny has always demonstrated respect and adoration for women."*

During a challenging period marked by illness, Weiss shared that Johnny was always there for him, underscoring his devotion. *"That shows what a true, loyal friend Johnny is."* Weiss told me *"Johnny was a generous person who was outnumbered by freeloaders, grifters,"* adding, *"I was one of the few friends in his life he knew that he could always count on."* He shared a startling insight: several of Johnny's supposed friends exploited his struggles with drugs and alcohol to cloud his judgment and pilfer from him. Despite Weiss' warnings about these opportunists who would steal valuable items and money right under his nose, Johnny remained non-confrontational. *"Ever since I've known Johnny, he has always been surrounded by people who pretend to be his friends while secretly taking advantage of him."*

As I delved deeper into the inner workings of the Viper Room, the name Big Ed Shaw came up repeatedly. Serving as the head bouncer from 1993 to 2004, he was a towering figure both in stature and reputation. Understanding his potential insight into the depths of the story I was exploring; I arranged a meeting with Big Ed. It began with palpable tension, his suspicion about my motives evident from the start. I didn't mince words; I openly informed him that I was conducting research for Amber Heard's legal team. Despite his awareness of the controversies surrounding Johnny Depp, Big Ed remained guarded, adamant he had nothing to offer.

Recognizing his reticence, I tried to bridge the gap. *"Big Ed, I understand your loyalty towards Johnny and the support he's extended to you and others over the years. If you could spare a moment to answer a few questions, it would be immensely helpful,"* I proposed, appealing to his sense of allegiance.

Big Ed eventually came around and opened dialog with me, but I couldn't delay the most pressing question: *"Have you ever witnessed Johnny Depp abusing or physically assaulting a woman?"* His response was swift and forceful. *"Hell no, man! I don't know who would even say that. Anyone that says JD ever hit a woman is out of their damn mind. They don't know what they're talking about,"* Big Ed declared, his assertion slicing through the tension between us.

This heated exchange seemed to break the ice. Gradually, he opened-up with even more details. *"The first day I met JD, he asked me to come work for him,"* Big Ed recalled with a touch of nostalgia. His narrative then took a somber turn as he discussed his life after the Viper Room. Plagued by narcolepsy throughout his adult life, his situation worsened after a tragic car accident left him paralyzed from the waist down. *"When JD found out about my accident and that I couldn't walk anymore, he kept me on the payroll,"* Big Ed disclosed, his undying loyalty to Johnny unshaken by his personal tribulations.

Our conversation shifted to Johnny's 2018 legal settlement with The Management Group, which illuminated a pattern of betrayal by those closest to him. Echoing Chuck Weiss' earlier sentiments, Big Ed agreed that a few within Johnny's inner circle were often the ones exploiting his kindness.

Big Ed recounted a harrowing incident at the Viper Room one night when club employee Paul Schindler and an alleged Italian mobster became embroiled in what began as a trivial dispute. The situation escalated quickly when guns were drawn. If not for Big Ed's swift intervention to defuse the situation, it might have ended tragically.

When Depp learned about the incident, his concern for the safety and security within the Viper Room increased significantly, prompting him to suggest bulletproof jackets for Big Ed and the other bouncers. Despite the *'Finding Neverland'* actor's good intentions, this proposal was met with resistance from Big Ed, who argued that such measures would create a fortress-like atmosphere, undermining the club's welcoming ambiance. *"We don't go around beating up on people,"*

Big Ed asserted firmly, advocating for a security approach that was non-aggressive. A claim I would soon discover was a stark contrast to the truth.

Throughout my conversations with Big Ed Shaw, the story began to unfold further, revealing a pattern of loyalty, protection, and betrayal that characterized the Viper Room's atmosphere. This narrative was filled with contrasts, juxtaposing the light of generosity and steadfast support against darker backdrops of exploitation and personal loss. This nuanced understanding illuminated the dual nature of Depp's role at the club— not merely as an owner but as a protector to those within his circle.

As evidenced by the dozens of audiotapes and countless pages of investigative notes I compiled, the overarching consensus from more than a hundred people I interviewed, from coast to coast and across the seas, echoed the positive portrayals of Johnny Depp. This included friends, associates, employees, like groundskeepers, mechanics, drivers and even relatives like Depp's cousin *Ilene*, who tearfully recounted how Johnny paid off the mortgage after her husband fell on hard times.

Johnny Depp's Accidental Fixer

By mid-August 2019, the investigation led me to two pivotal figures whose insights enriched the complex narrative of the story: *New York Times* bestselling author Mark Ebner, who had extensively covered celebrity and crime culture for publications like *Spy*, *Rolling Stone*, and *Los Angeles Magazine*, and Rocky Leonard George, renowned guitarist for the band Fishbone. Both offered perspectives that diverged significantly from the prevalent narratives.

Each conversation illuminated different aspects of the Viper Room, peeling back its glamorous façade to expose the underlying dynamics that shaped its history. They also provided a more nuanced portrait of Johnny Depp, depicting him as a significant figure in a world where fortunes can change swiftly and unpredictably, and where Hollywood's bright lights often cast ominous shadows.

In 1997, Mark Ebner, then an investigative journalist for *Premiere Magazine*, found himself at a high-profile event at the Viper Room. The occasion was a celebration for Hunter S. Thompson's film, *'Fear and Loathing in Las Vegas'* attended by notables such as Johnny Depp and actor John Cusack.

I met with Ebner at the Pier Grill in Pasadena for a seafood lunch to discuss the event. He described his attempt to question Thompson about the film's tumultuous pre-production, only to be met with disdain. The situation escalated when Depp, in defense of Thompson, half-jokingly, threatened to *"set Ebner on fire."* Instead, Thompson opted to have Ebner physically thrown out, a moment that starkly revealed the undercurrents of aggression and exclusivity at the club. Ebner's attempt to re-enter surreptitiously ended with him being labeled a *"tabloid reporter"* by Depp and forcibly ejected once again by Big Ed and two other bouncers, illustrating the lengths to which the Viper Room's elite would go to protect their sanctuary.

This entire episode, captured on camera, served as a chilling prelude to more sinister revelations. Ebner later alleged that Depp played a role in his dismissal from the assignment, indicating the considerable influence that Depp wielded early in his career, highlighting the power dynamics and covert operations within the Viper Room.

The aggression displayed that night raises questions about Depp's tendencies towards violence. While the conclusions drawn and their use in Amber Heard's defense would be decided by her legal team, one cannot help but draw parallels. The threatening jest to set Ebner on fire echoes a disturbingly similar proposal Depp made

Johnny Depp's Accidental Fixer

sixteen years later in a 2013 text to his actor friend Paul Bettany. In the text, widely reported, Depp suggested, *"Let's burn her, [Amber]"* sinisterly adding, *"Let's drown her before we burn her, to make sure she's dead."* Such statements, regardless of their intent, painted a troubling picture of Depp's attitudes and actions.

Legal documents I uncovered in the underground archives of the West District Los Angeles Superior Court, disclosed a disturbing incident outside the Viper Room in 2003. The court filings revealed that Big Ed Shaw and three other club bouncers, Tim Wayne, Bob Brister and Teddy McClendon ambushed the iconic Fishbone guitarist Rocky Leonard George as he exited the club, subjecting him to a violent, unmerciful beating. This assault led to George filing a lawsuit against not only the four bouncers but also Johnny Depp and the Viper Room itself, citing charges of Assault and Battery and Negligent Hiring of Security.

George, who has a striking resemblance to the late Jimi Hendrix, became visibly shaken as he recounted the ordeal. George told me that on the early morning of September 12, 2001, just after 2 a.m., Big Ed vociferously ordered he and his friend, lead singer of the rock metal band 40 Cycle Hum, Brandon Mitchell, to leave the Viper Room because it was closing.

According to George, Big Ed was bullying and yelling at Mitchell for not moving quickly enough, resorting to insults, name-calling, and physical shoving. *"When I saw Big Ed grab Brandon by the arm and bully him, I intervened, and that's when Big Ed and the other bouncers decided to retaliate and turn their aggression against me."*

George stated that when the altercation spilled outside, the violence intensified. *"Big Ed and at least one other bouncer started punching me* and *then the others joined in."* George went on to say, *"They knocked me to the ground and kicked me in the face."* By the time the assault ended, the famed guitarist was left severely injured, battered, and bruised, with multiple broken teeth, and required hospitalization.

On November 21, 2003, Johnny Depp settled out of court with George for $13,500. Despite the settlement, Depp's decision to retain Big Ed and fire the three other bouncers implicated, spoke volumes about the club's internal dynamics and the loyalty networks that underpinned it. This decision, much like the rest of the Viper Room's storied existence, reflected a complex

Johnny Depp's Accidental Fixer

interplay of power, loyalty, and the shadowy lines between right and wrong.

Through interviews and court documents, a picture emerged of a place where the glitz and glamour of Hollywood nightlife were interwoven with undercurrents of violence, secrecy, and control. The Viper Room, it appeared, was not just a nightclub but a microcosm of the darker facets of celebrity culture and the lengths to which its operators and its patrons would go to protect their sanctuary.

As I closed my notebook and flicked off the lamp, the quiet of the early morning enveloped the room, offering a moment of deep reflection. Though the exploration of Depp's past was far from complete, these initial forays had established a solid foundation for the ongoing investigation. In the pursuit of truth, the past was proving to be more than just a silhouette looming in the background; it was a beacon, shedding light on the complexities of human behavior and the lasting impacts it can have on the present. This journey was only just beginning and the paths yet to be explored promised to reveal even more.

Chapter 6
The Rocky Road

My quest for a deeper understanding into Johnny Depp's complex character led me to a new figure, Gregg "Rocky" Brooks. His lawsuit against Depp alleged an assault during the filming of *'City of Lies'* an accusation that promised to shed new light on Depp's alleged propensity for violence. Obtaining his contact information and home address was the easy part, courtesy of a few well-placed industry contacts. Gaining his trust was another matter entirely. As the location manager on the film, Brooks had been integral to the day-to-day operations on set and his close involvement meant he had firsthand insights that were crucial to my investigation.

I informed Amber's lawyers that anyone on the *'City of Lies'* set during Brooks' alleged assault could be a key witness but cautioned that people might guard their careers and reputations closely. I explained the inherent risk in speaking out against Johnny Depp, emphasizing my approach to understand perspectives by placing myself in others' shoes. Given the prestige of working with Depp, I recognized their hesitation. *"Try your luck,"* Amber's lawyers encouraged, as I planned to first interview Brooks. The prospect of finding unimpeachable proof that Johnny is a violent man was of great interest to Amber and her legal team.

I initially emailed Brooks to outline my intentions and the scope of my investigation. His response was cautious and non-committal. It was clear that building rapport would take more than a straightforward inquiry. I decided a more personal approach was necessary. Less than twenty-four hours later, I arrived unannounced at his residence, knocking on his door, with a mixture of apprehension and determination. Mrs. Brooks, cautious yet curious, eventually opened the door. My introduction as Amber Heard's investigator was met with surprise and resignation. After a brief conversation, she agreed to pass my contact information to her husband.

To my astonishment, Brooks reached out the very next day. Our dialogue, initially cautious, evolved into an open exchange about his encounters with Depp. Gradually, he consented to meet. Amid an atmosphere of eager anticipation and the profound responsibility that lay before us, we scheduled our rendezvous for noon the next day at the Barclay Hotel in downtown Los Angeles-- the purported *"scene of the crime"* where Depp was alleged to have assaulted Brooks and where much of *'City of Lies,'* was filmed.

    I arrived at the Barclay Hotel an hour early the following day to ensure ample time to inquire whether any staff members were present during the filming of *'City of Lies.' Rudy*, the hotel's manager, a stocky, middle-aged Hispanic man with a friendly yet reserved demeanor, admitted he was frequently on duty during that period but hesitated to share details about Johnny Depp's conduct at the hotel. His attitude shifted when I proposed a financial incentive for his cooperation. Encouraged, after I handed him a crisp one-hundred-dollar bill, he began to divulge valuable insights. *"Johnny was always nice,"* he remarked, adding, *"I never witnessed anything out of the ordinary about him, during the numerous times our paths crossed."*

    Rudy recalled a particular encounter involving a mother and daughter who had met the renowned *'Sweeney Todd'* actor outside the hotel after Brooks' alleged altercation with Depp. After another monetary inducement Rudy provided me with the contact information for the mother whom I would later pursue.

Brooks arrived on time at our designated meeting spot, prepared to delve into the particulars of his lawsuit. Over a cup of black coffee, he talked about the intricacies of his legal struggles, the impact of his on-set experiences and the influence of Hollywood politics on his future as a movie locations manager. Brooks openly discussed the legal proceedings he was embroiled in and revealed how the alleged assault had severely affected his mental health, mentioning that he was undergoing psychotherapy, which based on my experience is par for the course in civil matters involving alleged physical assaults.

For the next hour, Brooks described his clash with Depp with intense clarity, voicing his exasperation with the alleged incident. He recounted the awkward moment when he had to inform Johnny, who was directing the final scene in *'City of Lies'* that he was out of time. Brooks insisted, *"This notification was the responsibility of the director, Brad Furman, who uncharacteristically gave it to me."*

Brooks depicted a bleak view of Hollywood politics, fearing that his career was at stake regardless of the lawsuit. I offered my support and then disclosed my primary involvement in the Depp v. Heard case, explaining that I was gathering evidence of Johnny's alleged violent behavior. Before he could respond, I pressed him for the names and contact details of anyone on the set who might have witnessed his alleged assault, stressing the need for concrete evidence.

Much to my surprise and delight, I assume motivated by a strong desire to hold Johnny accountable, Brooks reached into the folder he brought with him into the hotel and produced a series of documents. As he handed them to me, he stated, *"This is everything you'll need— production reports, names and contact numbers of the cast and crew, and daily production schedules."*

I was speechless as I clutched the stack of confidential movie production papers-- a treasure trove of potential evidence at my disposal, documenting eyewitness accounts of the alleged assault. Back in my home office, I forewent dinner but poured myself a glass of vino. I proceeded to meticulously sift through the *'City of Lies'* cast and crew list. I labored into the early hours, reducing the list of names to approximately 15 potential witnesses who had been within a 20-foot radius of the alleged assault on Brooks, just before midnight, on April 12, 2017.

Johnny Depp's Accidental Fixer

After a restless night, my morning routine of black coffee, two hardboiled eggs, did little to ease my mind, spurred on by thoughts of pursuing my fresh leads. Over the next several days, I reached out to the individuals on my list, eventually focusing on six potential witnesses. My initial call was to Brooks' personal assistant and primary witness, Miguel Gutierrez, who was keen to share his account. Miguel detailed how Johnny yelled at his boss, challenging him to punch him in the face and offering $100,000 if he did. Miquel added, *"I saw Johnny hit him twice in the lower torso."*

Next, I contacted Brad Furman, the director of *'City of Lies'* who vehemently denied any physical altercation, insisting he was only a foot away and refuted any claims to the contrary as false. Before 11a.m. the next day, I spoke with Jane Galli, head of the makeup department, who was present at the Barclay Hotel entrance during the incident. *"I was about ten feet away, and I can confirm there was no physical contact,"* she asserted, adding, *"I worked with Johnny on 'Public Enemies' and 'Pirates,' and he's always been delightful."*

Later in the afternoon, I interviewed the 1st Assistant Director, Paul Silver, who initially hesitated but eventually opened-up. I explained that my task involved profiling Johnny Depp's character and temperament, particularly in relation to the alleged assault on Rocky Brooks. Silver confirmed his awareness of the incident. He told me that he had been positioned across the street, about 15 to 20 feet away. He didn't see Johnny hit Brooks but did confirm that a heated verbal exchange had occurred between the two.

As our conversation deepened, it became clear that Silver had more to share, particularly regarding the film's director, Brad Furman. He characterized Furman as the true instigator behind the tensions during the movie's production. *"The real troublemaker was the director, Brad Furman,"* he asserted, adding, *"Brad was combative, inflexible and frequently clashed with everyone involved."*

Silver offered a detailed account on how Furman fueled the confrontation by instructing Brooks to deliver the bad news to Johnny that he would not be able to complete the final scene due to time constraints: *"Rocky Brooks was the film's locations manager. He had no business addressing the principal actors on such matters. It was squarely the director's responsibility."*

Silver also revealed that Furman's ongoing conflicts with the film's producer Miriam Segal had escalated to the point where she was barred from the set during Johnny's scenes. Seeking clarity on who initiated Segal's exclusion, Silver confirmed, *"It was Johnny who made that decision, not over personal grievances but due to her disputes with Brad,"* adding, *"Johnny, like many artists, is prone to being emotionally expressive. He was never unkind to Miriam, but he was straightforward."*

I asked Silver if there was anything about Johnny Depp that he found objectionable. He admitted that *"Johnny frequently arrived late. He did tend to arrive on his own schedule but it usually didn't disrupt the day's schedule too severely… Well, perhaps just a bit."*

I inquired of Silver whether there was any validity to the claims that the Los Angeles Police Department was deliberately hindering the release of *'City of Lies'* due to the film's critical depiction of the LAPD's Rampart Division and its supposed involvement in the 1997 assassination of rapper Biggie Smalls. *"Let's just say that the LAPD's interference, along with Rocky Brooks' lawsuit, were indeed contributing to delays in the film's release, and Brad was not pleased about it."*

I confided that Brooks had disclosed to me how he consistently detected the scent of alcohol on Johnny's breath throughout the filming of *'City of Lies.'* He particularly noted that on the evening of the alleged assault, the odor was unmistakably strong. Curious, I asked Silver if he had ever noticed the same. He laughed, *"I never got that close to Johnny to tell."*

Following up on Brooks' claim Johnny verbally abused a homeless black woman in the area, I asked Silver if there was any truth to this allegation. *"Absolutely not. If there's one thing, I can say about Johnny is that he consistently showed nothing but kindness and genuine empathy towards the homeless people we encountered while filming,"* adding, *"In fact, he often engaged in extended conversations with them, much to our team's impatience."*

Silver's insights provided a nuanced perspective on the *'Ed Wood'* actor's capacity to present a serene and approachable demeanor during public interactions. His streamlined account captures the essence of my investigative efforts, balancing the pursuit of truth with the complexities of Hollywood dynamics. Each conversation added to the Depp mystique, a man beloved by many for his charm, generosity, and kindness, yet shadowed by whispers of darker moments.

Before week's end, I received a call from Set Production Assistant Kara Ebensberger, who apologized for her delayed response, citing her exhaustive work schedule. Kara, who had been on the sidewalk across the street during the alleged incident, shared that she heard loud voices but couldn't make out the specifics of the conversation due to her obstructed view. When asked to describe Johnny Depp's demeanor during the filming she warmly replied, *"This might sound biased, but Johnny was lovely,"* adding *"The three weeks I spent working with him were thoroughly enjoyable."*

Rocky Brooks alleged that he sought LAPD intervention during his altercation with Depp. This claim was only partially accurate. My investigation found that he was referring to John David Bigrigg, a retired Los Angeles police officer whom, at the time, was working on the set with the Los Angeles Police Motion Picture Television & Film Enforcement Unit. He was stationed half a block away when the incident unfolded.

Following my interview with Bigrigg, I determined that he had managed to assess the situation between Depp and Brooks effectively and impartially, based on witness testimonies collected at the scene. His actions reflected the competence one might expect from a veteran officer who had served in the United States Army Special Forces as a Green Beret before his policing career. It became clear to me that Bigrigg was a reliable and honorable man.

Bigrigg provided insights into his role within the LAPD film unit, comprised of retired officers tasked with managing traffic. He elaborated, *"Our experience ensures the safety of running shots and stunts on city streets, enhancing the overall efficacy of production efforts. We get around on motorcycles,"* humorously adding, "Our role is *akin to the Victorian Guard—often overlooked but essential."*

"Ultimately," Bigrigg stated succinctly, *"based on what I gathered, neither party involved in the dispute showed any physical aftermath. There were no injuries, no harm done, and no one expressed interest in pressing charges."* The 30-year retried LAPD Sergeant described the confrontation between Depp and Brooks as a *"trivial quarrel,"* emphasizing, *"It did not result in any legal action, hospital visits, or arrests."* He pondered briefly before remarking on the rarity of physical confrontations between actors and crew members, sternly noting, *"There were no visible injuries on either individual involved."*

The inconsistencies among the narratives from those intimately involved in the film set underscored the complex task of reconstructing the true essence of the incident. Each testimony offered a distinct perspective, highlighting the intricate and often subjective nature of occurrences behind the scenes of a movie production. Upon examining the production report that Brooks provided, it became apparent that the making of *'City of Lies'* was plagued by a series of misfortunes, including bizarre accidents, injuries, and tragically, a fatality on the penultimate day of shooting.

The series of mishaps began on the first day when a sudden power outage led to assistant property master Jesse J. Adams known for his work on *'Fast & Furious'* and *'Made in America,'* sustained a head injury that required a to the hospital emergency room.

On the second day of shooting the film's van driver was involved in a rear-end collision; on the third day, lighting technician Dustin Gardner, with credits from *'Peppermint'* and *'Interstellar,'* suffered electrocution due to defective equipment amidst rainfall.

On the fifth day, a film truck collided with a trailer, followed by another vehicular crash involving a film van three days later. On the twelfth day, a background artist was hit by director Brad Furman's vehicle.

Four weeks into the shoot, Johnny Depp fell ill with a severe fever and sweats, rendering him too weak to work for several days.

The most devastating event occurred on the thirty-sixth day when Production Assistant Lester Williams, just one hour after working a sixteen-hour shift, was fatally injured by a drunk driver.

Despite undergoing emergency surgery, he passed away within three hours. The following day, April 12, 2017, late in the afternoon, and on the final day of filming, the gravity of Lester's demise profoundly affected the entire cast and crew. *Ray*, the elderly Barclay hotel security guard who I interviewed at length, told me that Lester's tragic end had a particularly deep impact on Johnny, casting a dark shadow over the final day of production.

Even with the prevailing sorrow and tension, my investigation found that Johnny displayed commendable professionalism, performing in multiple scenes before stepping in as director for the film's concluding sequence. Ray emphasized Johnny's professionalism, remarking that the confrontation he had with Rocky Brooks paled in comparison to the sorrow stemming from Lester's death.

Johnny Depp's Accidental Fixer

As I neared the conclusion of my investigation into the alleged assault on Brooks, I finally tracked down the mother and daughter that Rudy, the hotel manager, had tipped me off on. Elisa Ontiveros addressed inquiries regarding Johnny's supposed intoxication, sharing her close encounter during an autograph session. She described Johnny as *"very gracious, cool, calm, and collected,"* showing no signs of distress from any supposed dispute—a point she emphasized, noting she and her daughter Kiesha's unawareness of any altercation Johnny was alleged to have had with Brooks.

Dismissing Brooks' allegations of alcohol smell, Elisa asserted Johnny was sober. She recounted a meaningful 20-minute conversation that she and Kiesha had with Johnny, where *'The Lone Ranger'* star's respect and kindness shone through. Notably, Johnny took an interest in Elisa's hospital work and encouraged Kiesha, a college freshman, to *"chase her dreams"* with *"great confidence and determination."*

This investigation was more than just a quest for the truth about specific incidents; it was a journey into the heart of Hollywood, where fame and talent often clash with the realities of human behavior. Each witness each piece of evidence, added layers to the narrative, revealing the complexities of a man who had captivated audiences around the world.

At this stage of my investigation, I was reminded of the delicate balance between seeking justice and navigating the intricacies of human relationships. My journey through the allegations, the lawsuits and conflicting accounts were a testament to the search for truth in a world where perceptions often outweigh facts. This was not just an investigation into the actions of Johnny Depp; it was an exploration of the human condition, of the shadows that lurk behind the glittering façade of celebrity.

My investigation into the *'Don Juan DeMarco,'* actor and *'Adderall Diaries'* actress's rocky relationship and the allegations that stemmed from it was a reminder of the fragility of human nature. It was a journey that took me through the highs and lows of Hollywood, through the contradictions and confessions that define our search for truth. I was left with a deeper understanding of the challenges that lie in discerning fact from fiction in a world where appearances can be as deceptive as they are compelling.

This realization struck a chord with me, underscoring the critical importance of discerning fact from opinion, especially in a case as convoluted and publicized as this one. The challenge was not merely to gather evidence but to sift through the cacophony to find the signal that could lead me to the truth.

This episode was a stark reminder of the pitfalls that come with investigating public figures. The line between evidence and inference can be razor-thin and the pressure to find conclusive proof can sometimes lead to overzealous interpretations. As I continued my investigation, I remained guided by a commitment to never lose sight of the responsibility that came with unraveling the truth behind the headlines.

It was more than a quest for evidence; it was an exploration of the delicate interplay between fame, power and the human condition. Each step forward was a step into the unknown, with the only certainty being my unwavering commitment to uncovering the truth, wherever it may lead. The investigation was not just about proving or disproving allegations; it was about understanding the intricacies of human relationships and the shadows that fame can cast on the truth.

Chapter 7
Unraveling the Tangled Web

On the morning of August 8, 2019, I sat across from Jonathan Shaw, a renowned figure in the world of tattoo artistry. We were in a simple, unassuming setting, but the conversation that unfolded carried a significant weight. A counterculture icon and long-time friend of Johnny Depp, the ink master's complex character reflected the multifaceted relationships that define much of Hollywood's inner circles.

Shaw had a past marred by weapons charges. In 2010 he was arrested in New York City for allegedly attempting to ship a loaded AK-47 assault rifle, three other guns, 68 illegal knives and more than 2800 rounds of ammunition. He claimed it was a calculated set up: *"When I got back from Brazil after 9/11 the laws had changed. I went through an ordeal, but I had the best criminal lawyers. The whole thing eventually went away."*

Johnny Depp's Accidental Fixer

Born into a world of show business, Shaw's father was the famous band leader and clarinetist Artie Shaw, famously known for his 1938 recording of Cole Porter's *'Begin the Beguine.'* His mother, Doris Dowling, was a noted actress, known for the films, *'The Crimson Key'* and *'Bitter Rice.'* Despite this background in entertainment, Shaw carved out his own distinct path, gaining prominence as a tattoo artist in NYC, where he established himself as a pioneer in the industry. In 1976, he founded New York's first tattoo parlor Fun City-- when tattooing was still illegal.

A living legend in the field of body ink artistry, Shaw is best known for his neo-tribal tattoos, distinctive style, blending traditional American tattoo motifs with his unique vision and customary skull and crossbones. *"My tag is the skull and crossbones. Johnny really liked the skull and crossbones so the one you see on his arm, I did."* There was a hint of pride in his voice, a testament to the bond they shared, immortalized in ink.

Apart from his tattooing career, Shaw is also an accomplished writer and novelist who draws upon the gritty underbelly of society for inspiration. His writing, as in the *Narcisa: Our Lady of Ashes*, is recognized for its raw, unfiltered portrayal of the darker aspects of human nature and society.

Depp, known for his own appreciation of the tattoo culture, found a kindred spirit in Shaw. Their friendship, spanning decades, has been marked by mutual respect and shared artistic sensibilities. Shaw spoke of a life lived in the fringes of society and his friendship with Depp. *"I knew Johnny long before he became a famous actor,"* he reminisced, his voice tinged with nostalgia.

The unwavering love and loyalty Shaw held for his dearest friend was undeniable. *"Johnny is super controlled, super kind, and a superhuman being."* Shaw's demeanor reflected a mix of reverence and affection for Depp. *"I've never seen Johnny lose it—lose his temper. He has always been a really gentle guy."* There was an earnestness in his tone, one that seemed to plead for the truth of his words to be understood.

In September 1994 the gossip rags had a field day when Depp trashed his room at the Mark Hotel in NYC. It was rumored that his then girlfriend, supermodel Kate Moss, was injured during the melee. *"Look, we all get angry,"* Shaw insisted, adding, *" Johnny didn't bust up a live person, he busted up inanimate objects. He didn't hurt Kate, only things, big difference."*

It was clear Shaw viewed Depp's actions through a lens of empathy and understanding. *"The Johnny I knew was always a caring, gentle guy."*

The conversation inevitably steered towards the widely publicized lawsuit involving Amber Heard. Shaw's expression turned somber. The tirade he unleashed against Johnny's ex-wife was harsh and unfiltered, reflecting the polarized views surrounding the Depp-Heard saga. Shaw's animosity towards Amber Heard was palpable, his language painting such a vivid picture of his disdain for her sent a chill up my spine: *"The only thing I would be willing to help that gold-digging whore do is help load the gun she wanted to use to blow her fucking brains out."*

Writer, actress Stacey Grenrock-Woods, who is best known for her role as the Fox News reporter in *'Arrested Development'* stated, *"The thought that Johnny would ever strike a woman or physically assault anyone is so foreign to me."* The former model and correspondent for the *Daily Show* was noticeably stunned by my inquiry. *"I have not heard from Johnny for several years but if he ever hit a woman, I would have remembered,"* adding, *"Johnny has always shown affection and tenderness toward women, including myself."*

Renowned actor Xander Berkeley who has been featured in over 200 films and television projects like *'Terminator 2: Judgment Day,' 'Air Force One'* and most recently with Depp in *'City of Lies'* told me that he had known Johnny for decades. *"Johnny is kind, unassuming and nonconfrontational."* Adding, *"I consider him a friend. He's a consummate professional and I loved working with him."*

Xander, who is also an accomplished painter, did not mince words. From the moment he opened his mouth, I knew he was as tough in real life as he is in the strong-arm characters he portrays. *"I got to tell you, you seem like a nice guy, but if you're trying to dig some dirt up on Johnny, you're not gonna get it from me."*

In the world of Hollywood, where public appearances are carefully curated, such candid and serious-minded responses spoke volumes. It was a reminder of the complex web of relationships and reputations that I was navigating.

Chapter 8
Baruch the Mooch

By this time in the landscape of celebrity legal battles, only few have commanded as much attention and public scrutiny as the explosive lawsuit between Johnny Depp and Amber Heard.

At the heart of this legal storm was not just a feud over allegations and reputational damage but also a backstage drama filled with strategic shifts and unexpected turns in legal representation. I delved deep into the mechanics of these changes, revealing the critical maneuvers and personal dynamics that shaped the course of this high-profile case.

In an unexpected development, Amber's lawyers Eric George and Rick Schwartz, hinted at their withdrawal from the starlet's defense. Throughout my investigation, my efforts to tilt the scales in Amber's favor did not wane. Irrespective if Amber was contemplating hiring a new legal team, it was of no consequence to me. I was tasked to do a job and until I heard otherwise, I remained laser focused and absolutely committed to getting the job done.

———— ⚖ ————

When Johnny Depp's longtime friend Isaac Baruch was about to be scheduled for deposition, Schwartz gave me my marching orders: *"I want you to get me everything you can on him."*

Baruch was born on May 22, 1961, in Brooklyn, New York. During his early teens, his mother, Carmen, relocated the family to Surfside, Florida. Baruch attended Miami Beach High School, and in 1978, at 17, he formed the South Florida punk rock band, The Reactions.

According to one of his peers, Baruch was remembered as *"a wannabe rockstar; immature for his age."* The friend noted that while others pursued higher education or careers following high school, *"Isaac kinda bounced around like a nowhere man,"* adding, *"Not the ideal big brother figure for Johnny Depp."*

A testament to his immaturity was evident in the pre-trial deposition Baruch gave in November 2019. During the deposition he candidly boasted of having engaged in

Johnny Depp's Accidental Fixer

a *"pissing and vomiting contest with Johnny to see who could pee and throw up the farthest."*

Baruch's enduring adolescent behavior was also highlighted when he recounted a time when Amber yelled at him to stop singing about diarrhea. This was understandable because Amber was cooking, but Baruch still needed to squawk: *"Amber yelled like nobody has ever yelled before."* Then, without warming, he unashamedly sang the song aloud for everyone in attendance: *"When you're running to first and your shorts are gonna burst, diarrhea, diarrhea. When you're going around third and you feel a wetty turd, diarrhea, diarrhea."*

Contrary to countless reports that Baruch and Depp were childhood friends, he was 19 and Depp was 17 when they first met. The two bonded over their mutual love of punk rock and playing in garage bands. At the time, Johnny was playing for his own band, The Kids. They traveled and performed in the same circles in Miami Beach, where nightclub gigs were scarce.

In 1980, when Baruch was looking for a bass guitarist for The Reactions, and Johnny Salton, known for floated above everyone else in skill, was available. He began developing a huge fan base since the 1970's and had a reputation for being quite a treat for the ladies. Baruch knew Salton's immense popularity and presence on stage would almost guarantee The Reactions instant success.

A little-known fact: During Salton's initial meeting with Baruch on joining the band, he expressed his interest in playing lead guitar, but Baruch insisted that he was the lead guitarist. He told Salton, under no uncertain terms, that if he came on board, he'd have to settle for playing bass. Salton accepted but with the caveat that if another opportunity came along that was more befitting of a musician with his talents, he'd likely have to part ways. Baruch took the gamble; one he would arguably regret.

In 1981, Salton began to lose interest in performing with The Reactions because they didn't have enough songs and had to resort to playing the same tunes ad nauseam. Understandably, when he got an offer to play with Charlie Pickett and the Eggs, he took it, and soon thereafter, The Reactions disbanded. Following the breakup, Baruch relocated to California where his attempts to establish other bands, like U.S. Fury's and Revolver floundered.

Baruch's move to the west coast ushered in some run-ins with the law. Criminal arrest filings reveal he was incarcerated on June 12, 1981, for possession of controlled substance. It was no surprise decades later he would testify in Depp v. Heard that he not only saw Depp do drugs, but he had also *"partaken."*

In June 2018, Johnny sued *News Group News*, the company publishing *The Sun, UK* for libel. He claimed that *The Sun's* goal was to convince its readers that he was a *"wife beater"* and should be dropped from the '*Fantastic Beasts*' franchise.

Baruch submitted a witness statement to the High Court of Justice on Depp's behalf. In his statement he was unseemly critical of Amber for the way she handled her split with Johnny. In the declaration, Baruch smugly asserted, *"I really thought Amber had more integrity and emotional understanding of her own resentments toward Mr. Depp to avoid going through a divorce in the manner she was."* This was rich coming from someone who had struggled with his own failed marriage.

Evident in legal filings I obtained from the Superior Court of Los Angeles archives, in April 1989, Baruch married aspiring nurse, Darcie, separated just four months later and subsequently divorced. He stoneheartedly characterized his brief union with Darcie as, *"being married once for about three minutes."*

On August 17, 2019, I interviewed Darcie who said, *"My marriage with Isaac started out okay, but toward the end it got pretty bad,"* adding, *"I'm a nurse now and so the thing is, people have triggers in their lives, and they're called 'gas lighters.'"* I asked if she meant Isaac was controlling and manipulative. *"Well, let's just say he has a personality."*

I confided that I was investigating Depp, but I was also interested in knowing about the people he associated with. Darcie remarked, *"I get it. Birds of a feather flock together."*

I asked Darcie if she could give me a bit more insight on her ex-husband: *"Look, Paul, Amber is a very rich woman and I'm sure she is capable of helping herself. She's lucky that she didn't have to go to a women's shelter. Now if she was a poor woman on the street and struggling, maybe I would think twice about helping her."*

I told Darcie I had interviewed dozens of Johnny's closest friends and former employees and so far, not one of them had anything bad to say about him.

Darcie remarked, *"Well, I think it goes a little deeper for Isaac because Johnny is his benefactor."*

"That's true," I said, *"By all accounts, Johnny's been his meal ticket for years."*

"Good!" Darcie shouted, *"I hope he's rich now so I can take all his money."*

In 1993, with his prospects of making it in music fading, Baruch turned to Depp, who by now was an accomplished actor and proprietor of the Viper Room. Recognizing his old friend's dire circumstances, Johnny compassionately hired Baruch to work as a barback at the club.

In the early 2000's the *'Fear and Loathing in Las Vegas'* star transferred his ownership stake in the club to his former business partner Anthony Fox's daughter, Constance. He gave his former employees the option to continue working at the club or leave with a generous stipend. Baruch took the money.

During the Depp v. Heard trial, Baruch alleged that he used the severance pay to pursue a degree in art, but by 2012, he was still no better off. *Generous Johnny*, or some might say, *Johnny the enabler*, came to Baruch's rescue once again, allowing him to live rent-free in one of his multimillion-dollar penthouses in downtown Los Angeles. This is when Johnny officially became Baruch's benefactor, covering all his expenses, on the condition he *"Just paint."*

Because of the homoeroticism depicted in his paintings-- one of which depicts Donald Trump performing fellatio on five well-endowed men, I contacted Baruch via Facebook, on the pretext of hiring him to paint gay erotic t-shirts. He never responded.

During his November 2019 deposition, Amber's then lawyer John Quinn, asked Baruch, *"You've never been in an intimate or romantic relationship with Mr. Depp, right?"* Uncomfortable with the inquiry, blushing Baruch made a futile attempt to control the narrative by exploding: *"Hang on a second, because even to ask that question-- All that comes from the paintings that I have."*

Baruch continued his rant, attacking me: *"This guy Paul Barresi, who worked for you cats, tried to fishhook me."* Without fact or basis, he then proceeded to falsely accuse me of *"blackmailing, harassing,"* and *"scaring"* witnesses.

At trial, Baruch testified he was angry with Amber for telling *"malicious lies"* -- a fault he shares with her. Amber's lawyer questioned Baruch *"whether there ever*

Johnny Depp's Accidental Fixer

came a time he thought about paying Johnny back for his generosity." Baruch pitiably testified: *"The only thing I got is paintings,"* but swore that if *"this stuff* [his paintings] *ever sells,"* he'd split the proceeds with Johnny 50/50, emphasizing, *"And I ain't taking no for an answer—I gotta put something into this."*

Baruch may have been entertaining on the stand, but he also proved he had a knack for making false promises and telling tall tales. My investigation found that upon his mother's death in July 2018- when Depp was at the apex of his financial struggles- Baruch and his sister inherited their mother's Florida coastline estate, valued today at $1,250,000.

This additional asset disclosed in his mother's Last Will and Testament was yet another window into Baruch probable financial standing, starkly contrasting the courtroom narrative of the starving artist.

The intriguing facts that I uncovered about the man who took advantage of Johnny's generosity for decades, was far from the sympathetic character Depp's legal team so brilliantly staged.

Paul Barresi

"I don't blame people for who they are, only pretending to be what they are not."

⚖

Baruch the Mooch - "All I have is my paintings."

Johnny Depp's Accidental Fixer

2/10/2020 2:28 PM FILED FOR RECORD

Last Will and Testament 19-5274CP01
– of –
CARMEN BARUCH

I, CARMEN BARUCH of Dade County, in the State of Florida, do hereby make, publish and declare this to be my Last Will and Testament, hereby revoking all other Wills and Codicils at any time heretofore made. - - - - - - - - - - - - - - -

ARTICLE I

I nominate and appoint my daughter LEA BARUCH as the Personal Representative of my Estate without the necessity of posting bond. I hereby confer upon my Personal Representative full authority and power in her discretion, and without court order:

(a) To retain all or any part of my Estate in the form in which it exists at my death, notwithstanding that the same may not be permitted by law, for investment by fiduciaries. --

(b) To sell or otherwise dispose of all of my real and personal property at public or private sale, with or without notice. ---------------------------------------

(c) To make good and sufficient conveyance to any purchasers and until property is sold or otherwise disposed of, to rent the same for such period or periods as may seem advisable and collect the income and proceeds therefrom. ---

(d) To borrow money for the use of my Estate without security or on such security as may be necessary. ------------------

(e) To exercise all rights, including voting and subscription with respect to any securities of my Estate. --------------

ARTICLE II

I direct that all of my just debts and funeral and administration expenses be paid as soon after my death as is practicable. - - -

ARTICLE III

Following the payment of my just debts and funeral expenses I give and bequeath my entire Estate whether real, personal or mixed to my children LEA BARUCH and ISAAC BARUCH share and share alike for and during their natural lives. ---------
In the event either one of my children shall predecease the other I direct that share of my Estate which such child would have taken shall be given to the survivor. - - - - - - -

Carmen Baruch - Last Will and Testament

Chapter 9
Roots of Resilience

As the summer heat of August pressed down upon me, the weight of my investigation into Johnny Depp's background grew heavier with each passing day. Delving into the deep waters of Hollywood's secrets, my search for the truth took me on a journey far beyond the glitz and glamour, back to the Depp family roots. It was a saga of struggle, resilience, and ambition—woven from the humble beginnings of Depp's ancestors that had remained hidden from the public eye.

Johnny's maternal lineage painted a picture of hardship and perseverance. His mother, Betty Sue Wells, was born into the poverty-stricken world of Kentucky coal mines. The story of her life, set against the backdrop of the 1950s, paints a vivid picture of the societal norms and economic conditions of the era. Born into the adversity that often accompanies necessity, Betty Sue's family faced the universal challenges associated with financial hardship. Yet, this environment did not hinder her elder brother Bill, who rose above these challenges to become a Floyd County, Kentucky Executive Judge. This was a testament to the resilience and determination that seemed to run in the family.

When Betty Sue turned eighteen on January 1, 1953, she was aware of the gender-based limitations in career opportunities during that period in America. The era was characterized by a stark division in job roles, with *"women's jobs"* limited to teaching, nursing, librarian, secretary, waitress, factory worker, or store clerk. Higher education for women was not widely encouraged and if pursued, it was often seen as a pathway to matrimony rather than a career.

Betty Sue prioritized financial security in her choice of a partner, leading her into a relationship with John Dale Jr., a World War II Navy veteran, nine years her senior. Following his military service, Dale Jr. became a police officer in Paintsville, Kentucky. After leaving law enforcement, he settled into a career position with the Kentucky West Virginia Gas Company which promised the stability she sought. Betty Sue's marriage with him began in the spirit of traditional courtship and bore fruit with the birth of their first child, Daniel, on November 24, 1953. Their baby girl Deborah followed three years later. Despite their initial unity, the marriage eventually unraveled, leaving Betty Sue with custody of their children.

In stark contrast to Betty Sue's modest upbringing, John Depp Sr., along with his siblings Larry, Virginia, and Bob, were born into an environment of privilege, wealth and social esteem. The Depp family enjoyed a high social standing which afforded them many opportunities and comforts. When John Sr. first laid eyes on Betty Sue in 1960, her beauty struck him immediately. Despite objections from his family and the social complexities of marrying a woman with children from a previous marriage, John Sr.'s affection for Betty Sue was unshakeable. He chose to follow his heart and proposed to her.

By the age of twenty, John Sr. was already well-established in his career as a construction engineer. This position not only showcased his early ambition but also his capacity to provide for a family—a characteristic that undoubtedly appealed to Betty Sue, given her own values and upbringing. Her resilience in the face of poverty and John Sr.'s resolve despite his family's wealth created a unique dynamic. Betty Sue valued stability and security, traits that John Sr. could offer. Their union was a fusion of two different worlds: her tenacity and determination born from a life of hardship, and his confidence and assurance nurtured in an environment of privilege.

This union set the stage for the legacy that their son, Johnny, would inherit. The blend of Betty Sue's strength and John Sr.'s determination provided Johnny with a diverse heritage which he would build upon in his own life and career. The complexities of their backgrounds and their unwavering commitment to each other, laid a foundation of resilience and ambition that would come to define Johnny Depp's path to success.

From his earliest days, John Sr. harbored a dream that was deeply ingrained in his very being—the dream to become an engineer. This ambition wasn't a fleeting childhood fantasy but a steadfast goal, fueled by the legacy of his family and the values they upheld. As a graduate of Owensboro High School, where he excelled academically and distinguished himself as a dedicated member of the R.O.T.C. rifle team, John Sr.'s aspirations extended far beyond the typical expectations of his peers. His passion for engineering was more than just an interest; it was a calling, seemingly inscribed in his DNA.

His journey from aspiring engineer to accomplished professional was not just a personal achievement but a continuation of his family's legacy. As John Sr. transitioned from an apprentice to a respected engineer, his path reflected a deep-seated belief in the importance of following one's passion, a belief that would echo through the generations of the Depp family.

Johnny's grandfather, the venerable Oren Laramore Depp Sr. was the patriarch of the Depp family. Known affectionately as O.L., he was born on January 28, 1905. His move to Owensboro in 1936 marked the beginning of a significant chapter for the Depp family, one that intertwined with the fabric of American history and the personal trials and triumphs of its members.

O.L.'s early career saw him contributing to the community as the assistant district engineer for the Works Progress Administration [WPA] in Daviess County, a role he left behind to serve his country in World War II. His military service was distinguished, serving in the southwest Pacific with the 836th Combat Engineers Aviation Battalion and returning as a Lieutenant Colonel. Post-war, his efforts in organizing the National Guard Unit were pivotal, reflecting his commitment to service beyond the battlefield. The post-

Johnny Depp's Accidental Fixer

war era brought transformative changes to Owensboro, with O.L. playing a crucial role in transitioning the town from its modest industrial roots to a thriving community.

The establishment of Depp Contractor Co. in 1948 further underscored O.L.'s influence in shaping the landscape of Owensboro, a legacy that continued until his passing in 1979. His contributions laid a foundation of innovation and progress, turning Owensboro into a symbol of prosperity and growth. His vision and leadership left an indelible mark on the community, reflecting the potential of dedicated civic engagement and entrepreneurship. O.L.'s ventures into consulting engineering with J. Sam Johnson, followed by a partnership and vice-presidential role at Johnson, Depp and Quinsenberry, were instrumental in this transformation.

The union of John Depp Sr. and Betty Sue Dale on February 16, 1960 in Owensboro, Kentucky marked the merging of two distinct life paths. John Sr's. adoption of Betty Sue's children, Daniel age seven and Deborah, age four, symbolized the formation of a new family unit-- one that would soon include their own biological children. Christi, came along ten months after they married and Johnny, was born June 9, 1963. John Sr.'s professional journey, advancing from an assistant manager position for the city of Lexington, Kentucky to city manager, provided a stable foundation for his growing family.

Beneath the surface of this stability, turbulent currents flowed within the household. Betty Sue, a woman of strong will and emotional complexity, became an increasingly dominant force within the family.

As I delved into the intricacies of the Depp family history, it became evident that Betty Sue's struggles with her emotional wellbeing were profound, significantly influencing her relationships and the overall family dynamic. Her frequent treatments for her erratic behavior posed considerable challenges for Johnny, his father and his siblings to navigate. Betty Sue's bouts with depression and mood swings, often exacerbated by the pressures of raising a growing family, created a volatile environment.

Johnny's mother's instability would ultimately weave its way into the narrative in the Depp v. Heard trial. Contrary to the villainous portrait of Betty Sue being solely responsible for the family breakup, my investigation found that Johnny's father also played a significant role.

Johnny Depp's Accidental Fixer

During the Depp v. Heard courtroom drama, Johnny testified that his family moved frequently because of his mother, or rather, the *"fire in her feet."* While this may have been partially true, I discovered that the primary driver behind the frequent relocations was his father's struggle to find steady work.

Johnny was only six years old when a negative story about his father was published in The Corbin Kentucky Sunday Times: *"<u>Debate over Duties</u>: Frankfort Fires City Manager."* The cause was purportedly due to a contentious budget proposal by Frankfort, Kentucky's then city manager, John Depp Sr. which suggested increasing taxes. The loss of his job caused financial hardship, further straining the Depp family's emotional stability. Evidence also suggests Johnny's father had a wondering eye for the ladies, and a DUI arrest and conviction suggests a likely predilection for alcohol.

In June 1977, John Sr. relocated the family to Broward County, Florida where he purchased a modest three-bedroom home in Pembroke Pines-- a safe community near beautiful parks, excellent schools and shopping areas. In April 1979 he was appointed as the Utilities Director for the City of Pembroke Pines.

It seemed the family had finally begun to flourish. Unfortunately, this newfound stability was short-lived. Just two months before his sixteenth birthday, Johnny came home one-afternoon to discover, without warning, his father had left.

During the Depp v. Heard trial, Johnny's masterful legal team Ben Chew and Camille Vasquez set the stage to cast the blame on Betty Sue's abuse for driving his father away. The *'Pirate's'* star even offered a dramatic reenactment of his mother's zombie-like state during a failed suicide attempt after his father walked out because he *"just couldn't take it anymore."*

Johnny's gripping testimony highlighted Betty Sue's aggressive, mercurial and malevolent nature, drawing parallels to Amber. Conversely, his depiction of his father as the battered husband and victim, resonated with the jury, suggesting similarities with Johnny himself.

However, what I uncovered starkly contradicted the courtroom narrative. The circumstances surrounding Johnny's father's sudden departure and Betty Sue's failed suicide attempt was due to his love for another woman.

Evidence suggests, shortly after taking on his new job with the City of Pembroke Pines, Johnny's father fell in love with co-worker and former high school beauty queen, Marsha Johnson.

These findings not only highlighted the complexities and multifaceted nature of the Depp family's dynamic, but also illustrate that the roots of the Depp family's difficulties, extended beyond Betty Sue's mental health challenges. The rapid succession of events that followed marked the beginning of a series of complex developments that arguably had a profound impact on Johnny's life in unexpected ways.

John Sr. proposed to Marsha, and quit the dream job that earned him $25,000, a year, well above the average annual income at the time. In the span of three months, he sold the family home and sorted out a settlement agreement with Betty Sue. During this time Johnny was still a minor which raised concerns for family court Judge John G. Ferris who inquired, *"What about your minor son."* Betty Sue declared Johnny was self-sufficient, Despite the absence of a court filed certificate of emancipation, the judge took her at her word.

Johnny's father set the date to marry Marsha, on September 26, 1981. Betty Sue was not about to let him walk down the aisle with another before she did. She proposed to their family friend Bob Burt, and on June 12,

1981, just eight days after divorcing Johnny's father, Betty Sue and Bob Burt married.

I interviewed Bob Burt's daughter Adele who stated, *"Betty Sue asked him to marry her only to make John Sr. jealous,"* adding, *"But her scheme backfired."* Adele went on to say, *"When my father asked John Sr. if it was okay with him if he married Betty Sue, his response was 'Go for it!'* Adele said, *"This didn't go over well with Betty Sue. She didn't love my father, but she married my him anyway."* Adel confided that her father, being the kind and good-natured man that he was, *"couldn't bear to see Johnny homeless, so after he and Betty Sue were married, he invited Johnny to move in with them."* Adele told me that her father's marriage to Betty Sue was a living hell: *'She would sit at home all day, eating bon bons and watching television, and when my father came home from a hard day at work, she'd make him put on her pink apron, cook dinner, and then after they ate, she'd make him wash the dishes and clean house."*

On a lighter note, Burt's younger daughter Ellen told me that when Johnny later became famous, she had a long-standing joke that she shared with her close friends: *"I slept in Johnny Depp's bed."* The reality was that whenever Ellen came home from college, Johnny would have to give up her old bedroom and sleep on the sofa. Ellen recalled memories of how Johnny would roll up a pack of cigarettes in his t-shirt sleeve, like the boys did in the 1950's." Adding, *"Johnny was cute but not my type and way too young for me."*

Burt's son David expressed disappointment that his famous stepbrother has never acknowledged his father. *"Johnny had no trouble acknowledging career criminal Robert Palmer,"* who was his mother's fifth and final husband.

My investigation revealed that Betty Sue and her 'Cinderella man' Bob Burt's marriage lasted only eighteen months. Johnny's father was working at his new job for the city of Hallandale and still married to Marsha when he fell in love with another co-worker, June Watts. Legal documents reveal in June 1983, he divorced Marsha, and just sixteen days later married June. They've been together ever since-- a glowing testament to the adage, *"Three is a charm,"*

Chapter 10
The Threads That Bind

In the intricate dance of fate and circumstance, it is often the threads of our past that reveal connections where we least expect them. This investigation into Johnny's life started as a mere professional endeavor but swiftly evolved into a profound exploration of shared human experiences. As I pieced together his story from interviews with those who knew him best, I couldn't help but marvel at the unexpected parallels that emerged between his journey and mine.

Each conversation added a stitch to the fabric of our intertwined narratives, highlighting the common paths we traveled. The simple task of tracing Johnny's past; it became a reflective odyssey, uncovering the deep resonance between two lives shaped by similar struggles, yet expressed in uniquely personal ways.

My initial steps in the investigation were thorough and exhaustive. I reached out to anyone who had ever crossed paths with Johnny—his family members, former lovers, colleagues, childhood friends, and even casual acquaintances. Everyone provided a unique fragment of his life, contributing a piece to the complex puzzle that was Johnny. As I meticulously collected and assembled these tidbits, the emerging picture began to resonate with a surprising familiarity.

This discovery was startling; it was as if each testimony not only illuminated aspects of Johnny's character but also mirrored my own experiences, echoing the challenges and environments that had shaped us both.

The parallels were uncanny—from the fractured family dynamics we both endured, to the ways we sought refuge from our home lives, each story deepened the sense of connection I felt. This investigation, which started as a professional inquiry transformed into a personal journey, uncovering the shared themes of resilience and escape that defined both Johnny's path and my own.

Johnny and I both emerged from the crucible of fractured childhoods and broken homes where the specters of physical and emotional abuse cast long shadows over our formative years. His father, a civil servant deeply embedded in the municipal machinery, mirrored my own father's bureaucratic entanglements.

The oppressive atmosphere of our homes was further darkened by alcohol, rage and substance abuse, a constant, unyielding presence that shaped our childhoods.

Our means of escape, though distinct in their expression, were underscored by a common need—to find solace, to carve out a space where we could breathe. For me, it was the physical exertion and competitiveness of sports, the adrenaline rush of hard-fought competition, and the quiet, meditative focus of drawing, painting and sculpting that provided a refuge from the chaos of life.

These activities allowed me to channel my energy and emotions into something constructive, creating a buffer against the world's pressures. Johnny found his freedom in the melodies and rhythms of music. His guitar became a sanctuary where he could lose himself in the harmonious waves of sound, each strum a step away from reality.

Johnny's journey took a dark turn when he sought solace in drugs. What began as an attempt to cope with pain and find relief from the emotional turmoil eventually led him down a path of addiction, clouding his once-bright artistic vision. I too went down a dark path with my entry into the world of hard-core film. Kim Kardashian, Pamela Anderson, Tommy Lee and Paris

Hilton may have brought porn into vogue but when I undressed for the camera it came with deep consequences—like being disowned by my family.

Despite the different paths Johnny and I chose, our escapes were driven by the same yearning for peace and a place where we could truly be ourselves, free from judgment and the weight of our struggles.

The harsh sting of my father's rebuke whenever he caught me drawing. *"You'll never get anywhere drawing pictures, dummy!"* His words, accompanied by a demeaning smack across my face, echoed the dismissive criticisms Johnny faced. Each shared anecdote of his struggles was like a reflection of my own experiences.

I was also ensnared in a storm of verbal aggression: the sting of name-calling the bite of cruel insults, and the chilling threats of abandonment that echoed in my mind long after they were uttered. Physical aggression wasn't foreign either—hitting, pushing, throwing things in fits of rage. Johnny meticulously monitored his parents' volatile emotions, a daily ritual of survival.

Like Johnny, *"Staying out of the line of fire,"* was a strategy I knew all too well. We both had one parent who wielded hostility like a weapon, their relentless torment searing into our young minds, leaving us distraught, anxious, and hopeless. Johnny's parents' ceaseless conflicts chipped away at his ability to concentrate in school just as my father's relentless tirades shattered my focus and peace.

I recall one evening my mother sitting at the kitchen table, staring blankly at the wall as my father raged about some trivial mistake. Nevertheless, my mother's love for him was unwavering. Likewise, Betty Sue loved Johnny's father deeply, despite the turbulent and often abusive nature of their relationship. Her enduring love, in the face of constant turmoil, mirrored the steadfastness of my own mother, who stayed with my father despite the relentless torment she endured.

This shared aspect of our lives—the resilience and undying love of our mothers—formed another striking parallel between Johnny and me. It was a testament to the complex, often painful bonds that tied our families together, underscoring the deep-seated emotional scars that shaped our identities.

Our mutual experiences and need for escape bridged the gap between us, creating a bond that transcended the superficial. It wasn't merely professional curiosity that propelled me forward but a profound, personal connection that guided my exploration into Johnny's life.

Johnny Depp's Accidental Fixer

I felt a deep empathy for his struggles and triumphs, understanding the pressures he faced and the choices he made. This personal connection allowed me to see beyond the public persona and media portrayals, giving me insight into the complexities of his character. It was this empathetic link that fueled my commitment to uncovering the true story of Johnny Depp, not just as a celebrity, but as a human being navigating the turbulent waters of fame, personal demons and the quest for authenticity.

Through this journey, I aimed to honor our shared humanity, shedding light on the man behind the myths and offering a narrative grounded in genuine understanding and compassion.

As I pieced together Johnny's narrative, the task became increasingly complex. The array of voices—from social media chatter to well-trafficked blogs and media commentaries—each offered a different perspective on him, creating a labyrinth of mirrors that reflected various aspects of his persona.

Many of the commentaries, particularly those defending Amber, delivered stories heavy with supposition and emotional bias. These accounts were peppered with tentative language, indicating interpretative leaps rather than factual recounting, unquestionably influenced by a commitment to the Me-Too movement.

Navigating through these narratives required a balance of skepticism and openness—qualities necessary not just for understanding Johnny, but for introspection about my own life. This exploration into Johnny's past was like walking through a gallery of distorted mirrors, where each reflection prompted a reassessment of my own past, my decisions, and the paths I chose.

My investigation into a man's life evolved into a profound journey of human experience. It's an exploration of how our pasts carve out our identities, how the adversities we face can mold us into figures of resilience and how, within the narratives of others, we can glimpse reflections of our own struggles and victories.

In the words of Aristotle: *"Knowing yourself is the beginning of all wisdom."* This wisdom became the undercurrent of my investigation. As I delved deeper into Johnny's life, I was not only seeking to unearth the truths hidden in his past but also striving to comprehend the reverberations within my own life.

Final reflections…

Growing up, my parents fought more than they loved. Every day felt like a fresh wound, slowly wearing me down. I yearned for those rare moments when they'd exchange a conversation, a smile, maybe even a kiss. Those days were a rarity, and I was trapped in a nightmare with no escape. My only refuge was at the movies or the boys club—anywhere that wasn't home, anywhere that spared me from their relentless clashes.

This domestic turmoil set the stage for my career as a Hollywood fixer. When Amber's legal team hired me to find out if Johnny was the abusive monster Amber claimed, I wanted to side with her like I had with my mother. But I had a job to do, and I couldn't let this shared history cloud my judgement—I had to stay focused on the issue at hand.

Reflecting on my investigation in Depp v. Heard, I wonder if Amber's lawyers overlooked key evidence that I unearthed highlighting the fragile nature of the truth in the legal system and the profound impact of bypassed details on justice. Despite my unwavering confidence in the thoroughness of my investigation, in the end I found no evidence to substantiate Amber's claims.

In April 2020, I gave the Daily Mail in the UK an exclusive story about the work I did on Amber's behalf: **AMBER HEARD HIRED A P.I. TO DIG UP DIRT ON JOHNNY DEPP, BUT THE FIXER SPOKE TO 100 PEOPLE WHO ALL *"COULDN'T SAY ENOUGH ABOUT HIS GENEROSITY AND TENDER HEART"*—THOUGH SOME HAD HARSH WORDS FOR THE ACTRESS.**

Following the publication of this story, I received an email from Johnny's lawyer Adam Waldman which read:

"Dear Mr. Barresi - Johnny appreciates that you come clean about him in the Daily Mail and actually so do I."

I continued publishing dozens of favorable stories about Johnny, based on my findings, in national and international publications.

Adam and I stayed in touch, and just before trial, he called to relay to me what Johnny had told him:

'When it's all over I won't be surprised if Paul Barresi ends up the hero.'

The End